COLLINS

Cyc in

EDINBURGH
& SOUTH EAST SCOTLAND

C000202300

HarperCollins*Publishers*

Published by Collins
An imprint of HarperCollins*Publishers*
77–85 Fulham Palace Road
London W6 8JB

First published 1999
Copyright © HarperCollins*Publishers* Ltd 1999
Maps © Bartholomew Ltd 1999

Routes compiled by Peter Hawkins.
Design by Creative Matters Design Consultancy, Glasgow.
Typeset by Bob Vickers.

Photographs reproduced by kind permission of the following:
Dennis Hardley pages 20, 22–3, 39, 41, 48, 51, 55, 59, 76, 78, 82, 89;
Image Bank page 31; Scotland in Focus pages 5, 8, 84, 86, 96, 101, 103;
Andy Williams pages 11, 28.

Printed in Scotland

ISBN 0 00 448915 2
99/1/14

CONTENTS

KEY TO ROUTES

Distances have been rounded up or down to the nearest 0.5km (mile).

Route colour coding

undemanding rides compiled specifically with families in mind
15–25km (10–15 miles)

middle distance rides suitable for all cyclists
25–40km (15–25 miles)

half-day rides for the more experienced and adventurous cyclist
40–60km (25–40 miles)

challenging full-day rides
over 60km (over 40 miles)

grande randonnée – a grand cycling tour
100km (60 miles)

 Routes marked with this symbol are off-road or have off-road sections
(includes well-surfaced cycleways as well as rougher off-road tracks)

Near Moffat

LOCATION MAP

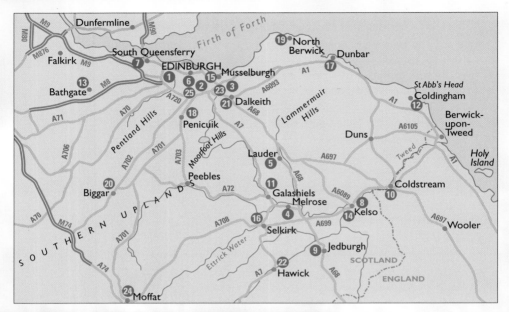

KEY TO ROUTE MAPS

M23	Motorway	Cycle route / Optional route	📞	Telephone
A259	'A' road / Dual carriageway	🚴 Start of cycle route	⊼	Picnic site
B2130	'B' road / Dual carriageway	⑫— Route direction	▲	Camping site
	Good minor road	Ⓑ Place of interest	👫	Public toilets
	Minor road	Public house	†	Place of worship
	Track / bridleway	Café / refreshments	🔆	Viewpoint
	Railway / station	✕ Restaurant	⌐	Golf course
	Canal / river	Convenience store	⁑	Tumulus
	Lake / loch	*i* Tourist Information Centre		Urban area
50	Contour (height in metres)	Ⓟ Parking		Woodland

Height above sea level

50	100	150	200	300	400	500	600	700	800	900 metres
165	330	490	655	985	1315	1645	1975	2305	2635	2965 feet

INTRODUCTION

How to use this guide

Collins' *Cycling in Edinburgh & South East Scotland* has been devised for those who want trips out on their bicycles along quiet roads and tracks, passing interesting places and convenient refreshment stops without having to devise their own routes. Each of the 25 routes in this book has been compiled and ridden by an experienced cyclist for cyclists of all abilities.

Cycling in Edinburgh & South East Scotland is easy to use. Routes range from undemanding rides compiled specifically with families in mind to challenging full-day rides; the type of route is easily identified by colour coding (see page 5). At the start of each route an information box summarises: total distance (in kilometres/miles – distances have been rounded up or down throughout to the nearest 0.5km/mile and are approximate only); grade (easy, moderate or strenuous based on distance and difficulty); terrain; an average time to allow for the route; directions to the start of the route by car and, if appropriate, by train.

Each route is fully mapped and has concise, easy-to-follow directions. Comprehensive information on places of interest and convenient refreshment stops along each route are also given. Accumulated mileages within each route description give an indication of progress, while the profile diagram is a graphic representation of gradients along the route. These should be used as a guide only.

The following abbreviations are used in the route directions:

LHF	left hand fork
RHF	right hand fork
SO	straight on
SP	signpost
TJ	T junction
TL	turn left
TR	turn right
XR	crossroads

Cycling in Edinburgh & South East Scotland

The rides in this book cover Edinburgh and South East Scotland, an area comprising West, East and Midlothian, and the Borders, with one foray to Moffat in Dumfries and Galloway, and another over the border to Flodden.

The routes are designed to stay away from busy main roads as much as possible and to allow cyclists to discover the peaceful back lanes, forestry tracks, bridleways and cycleways that cross this area, passing all manner of museums, castles, historic houses and other attractions.

If you are cycling one of the routes that starts in Edinburgh, you may find it useful to carry a Collins *Edinburgh Streetfinder*. Also, bear in mind that there is a wealth of attractions in the capital that you may wish to visit. Do allow yourself plenty of time to explore this magnificent city. Edinburgh Tourist Information Centre can provide comprehensive information on places to visit and things to do.

Some of the routes use sections of the National Cycle Network, which is being developed by the charity Sustrans, with the help of a £43.5 million grant from the Millennium Commission. The cycle network will run through towns and cities and link urban areas with the countryside. For further information on the National Cycle Network write to Sustrans, 35 King Street, Bristol, BS1 4DZ, telephone (0117) 926 8893, or visit their web site at www.sustrans.org.uk. Some routes also follow parts of the Tweed Cycleway, a signposted route on quiet minor roads, which runs for 145km (90 miles) between Biggar and Berwick-upon-Tweed. Traffic-free tracks, open to pedestrians and cyclists, are also used, some developed by local authorities and SPOKES, the Lothian Cycle Campaign which aims to encourage cycling and improve conditions for cyclists. SPOKES can be contacted on 0131 313 2114.

Geology, geography and history

Edinburgh, Scotland's capital, has a distinctive Old Town, superb museums and galleries, and ancient Edinburgh Castle. Edinburgh's oldest building stands within the castle walls – St Margaret's Chapel, built circa 1090 – around which the castle gradually developed. Holyrood Abbey was founded in 1128 and Edinburgh grew along the ridge between the abbey and the castle – the Old Town – narrow streets and tall, narrow buildings. With a general acceptance of the Union in Scotland came a period of prolonged peace and improved trade. The city of Edinburgh was extended with the creation of the New Town – broad, straight streets with low, wide buildings. Edinburgh's expansion eventually swallowed up neighbouring villages such as Cramond and Colinton.

Forth Rail Bridge

To the south of Edinburgh, rising above the fertile farmlands of East Lothian, lie the Pentland Hills – grassy hills used for livestock farming and the location of several reservoirs (part of Edinburgh's water supply). Scotland has comparatively few mineral resources and the land was traditionally used for agriculture. However, as coal-fuelled industry was developing during the 18th and 19th centuries, England's foreign markets opened up to Scotland and the large deposits of coal in West and Midlothian created new industries.

Beyond the Pentlands, in south east Scotland, are the Borders. For over 300 years, until after the unification of the Scottish and English crowns (1603) and parliaments (1707), this region was the scene of bloody conflicts, not only between the Scots and the English but between rival families. This is reflected in the surviving architecture – ruined abbeys and numerous fortified towers. The hills in the area are bounded by valleys, dissected by the narrow glens of rivers, and the plentiful water supply encouraged the development of textile manufacture. Most of the burns and rivers here are part of the River Tweed, which flows 161km (100 miles) from the Tweedsmuir Hills to Berwick, over the border in England.

Preparing for a cycling trip

Basic maintenance

A cycle ride is an immense pleasure, particularly on a warm sunny day. Nothing is better than coasting along a country lane gazing over the countryside. Unfortunately, not every cycling day is as perfect as this, and it is important to make sure that your bike is in good order and that you are taking the necessary clothing and supplies with you.

Before you go out on your bicycle check that everything is in order. Pump the tyres up if needed, and check that the brakes are working properly and that nothing is loose – the brakes are the only means of stopping quickly and safely. If there is a problem and you are not sure that you can fix it, take the bike to a cycle repair shop – they can often deal with small repairs very quickly.

When you go out cycling it is important to take either a puncture repair kit or a spare inner tube – it is often quicker to replace the inner tube in the event of a puncture, though it may be a good idea to practise first. You also need a pump, and with a slow puncture the pump may be enough to get you home. To remove the tyre you need a set of tyre levers. Other basic tools are an Allen key and a spanner. Some wheels on modern bikes can be removed by quick release levers built into the bike. Take a lock for your bike and if you have to leave it at any time, leave it in public view and locked through the frame and front wheel to something secure.

What to wear and take with you

It is not necessary to buy specialised cycling clothes. If it is not warm enough to wear shorts wear trousers which are easy to move in but fairly close to the leg below the knee – leggings are ideal – as this stops the trousers catching the chain. If you haven't got narrow-legged trousers, bicycle clips will hold them in. Jeans are not a good idea as they are rather tight and difficult to cycle in, and if they get wet they take a long time to dry. If your shorts or trousers are thin you might get a bit sore from being too long on the saddle. This problem can be reduced by using a gel saddle, and by wearing thicker, or extra, pants. Once you are a committed cyclist you can buy cycling shorts; or undershorts which have a protective pad built in and which can be worn under anything. It is a good idea to wear several thin layers of clothes so that you can add or remove layers as necessary. A zip-fronted top gives easy temperature control. Make sure you have something warm and something waterproof.

If you wear shoes with a firm, flat sole you will be able to exert pressure on the pedals easily, and will have less work to do to make the bicycle move. Gloves not only keep your hands warm but protect them in the event that you come off, and cycling mittens which cushion your hands are not expensive. A helmet is not a legal requirement, but it will protect your head if you fall.

In general it is a good idea to wear bright clothing so that you can be easily seen by motorists, and this is particularly important when it is overcast or getting dark. If you might be out in the dark or twilight fit your bicycle with lights – by law your bicycle must have a reflector. You can also buy reflective bands for your ankles, or to wear over your shoulder and back, and these help motorists to see you.

You may be surprised how quickly you use up energy when cycling, and it is important to eat a carbohydrate meal before you set out. When planning a long ride, eat well the night before. You should eat small amounts of food regularly while you are cycling, or you may find that your energy suddenly disappears, particularly if there are hills or if the weather is cold. It is important to always carry something to eat with you – chocolate, bananas, biscuits – so that if you do start fading away you can restore yourself quickly. In warm weather you will sweat and use up fluid, and you always need to carry something to drink – water will do! Many bicycles have a fitment in which to put a water bottle, and if you don't have one a cycle shop should be able to fit one.

It is also a good idea to carry a small first aid kit. This should include elastoplasts or bandages,

sunburn cream, and an anti-histamine in case you are stung by a passing insect.

It is a good idea to have a pannier to carry all these items. Some fit on the handlebars, some to the back of the seat and some onto a back rack. For a day's ride you probably won't need a lot of carrying capacity, but it is better to carry items in a pannier rather than in a rucksack on your back. Pack items that you are carrying carefully – loose items can be dangerous.

Getting to the start of the ride

If you are lucky you will be able to cycle to the start of the ride, but often transport is necessary. If you travel there by train, some sprinter services carry two bicycles without prior booking. Other services carry bicycles free in off-peak periods, but check the details with your local station. Alternatively, you could use your car – it may be possible to get a bike in the back of a hatchback if you take out the front wheel. There are inexpensive, easily fitted car racks which carry bicycles safely. Your local cycle store will be able to supply one to suit you.

Cycling on-road

Cycling on back roads is a delight with quiet lanes, interesting villages, good views and a smooth easy surface to coast along on. The cycle rides in this book are mainly on quiet roads but you sometimes cross busy roads or have stretches on B roads, and whatever sort of road you are on it is essential to ride safely. Always be aware of the possibility or existence of other traffic. Glance behind regularly, signal before you turn or change lane, and keep to the left. If there are motorists around, make sure that they have seen you before you cross their path. Cycling can be dangerous if you are competing for space with motor vehicles, many of which seem to have difficulty in seeing cyclists. When drivers are coming out of side

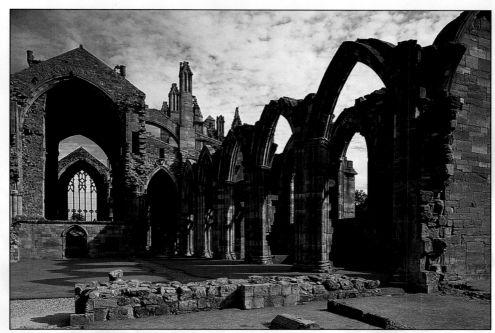

Melrose Abbey

roads, catch their eye before you ride in front of them.

You will find that many roads have potholes and uneven edges. They are much more difficult to spot when you are in a group because of the restricted view ahead, and therefore warnings need to be given. It is a good idea to cycle about a metre out into the road, conditions permitting, so that you avoid the worst of the uneven surfaces and to give you room to move in to the left if you are closely overtaken by a motor vehicle.

Other things to be careful of are slippery roads, particularly where there is mud or fallen leaves. Sudden rain after a period of dry weather often makes the roads extremely slippery. Dogs, too, are a hazard because they often move unpredictably, and sometimes like to chase cyclists. If you are not happy, stop or go slowly until the problem has passed.

Pedalling

Many modern bikes have 18 or 21 gears with three rings at the front and six or seven on the back wheel, and for much of the time you will find that the middle gear at the front with the range of gears at the back will be fine. Use your gears to find one that is easy to pedal along in so that your feet move round easily and you do not put too much pressure on your knees. If you are new to the bike and the gears it is a good idea to practise changing the gears on a stretch of flat, quiet road so that when you need to change gears quickly you will be ready to do so.

Cycling in a group

When cycling in a group it is essential to do so in a disciplined manner for your own, and others', safety. Do not ride too close to the bicycle in front of you – keep about a bicycle's length between you so that you will have space to brake or stop. Always keep both hands on the handlebars, except when signalling, etc. It is alright to cycle two abreast on quiet roads, but if it is necessary to change from cycling two abreast to single file this is usually done by the outside rider falling in behind the nearside rider; always cycle in single file where there are double white lines, on busy roads, or on narrow and winding roads where you have a restricted view of the road ahead. Overtake on the right (outside) only; do not overtake on the inside.

It is important to pass information to other members of the group, for example:

car up – a vehicle is coming up behind the group and will be overtaking;

car down – a vehicle is coming towards the group;

single up – get into single file;

stopping – stopping, or

slowing/easy – slowing due to junction, etc., ahead;

on the left – there is an obstacle on the left, e.g. pedestrian, parked car;

pothole – pothole (and point towards it).

Accidents

In case of an accident, stay calm and, if needed, ring the emergency services on 999. It is a good idea to carry a basic first aid kit and perhaps also one of the commercial foil wraps to put around anyone who has an accident to keep them warm. If someone comes off their bicycle move them and the bike off the road if it is safe to do so. Get someone in the party to warn approaching traffic to slow down, and if necessary ring for an ambulance.

Cycling off-road

All the routes in this book take you along legal rights of way – bridleways, byways open to all traffic and roads used as public paths – it is illegal to cycle along footpaths. Generally the off-road sections of the routes will be easy if the weather and ground are dry. If the weather has been wet and the ground is muddy, it is not a good idea to cycle along bridleways unless you do not mind getting dirty and unless you have a mountain bike which will not get blocked up with mud. In dry weather any bicycle will be able to cover the bridleway sections, but you may need to dismount if the path is very uneven.

Off-road cycling is different to cycling on the road. The average speed is lower, you will use more energy, your riding style will be different and there is a different set of rules to obey – the off-road code:

1 Give way to horse riders and pedestrians, and use a bell or call out to warn someone of your presence.

2 Take your rubbish with you.

3 Do not light fires.

4 Close gates behind you.

5 Do not interfere with wildlife, plants or trees.

6 Use only tracks where you have a right of way, or where the landowner has given you permission to ride.

7 Avoid back wheel skids, which can start erosion gulleys and ruin the bridleway.

Some of the off-road rides take you some miles from shelter and civilisation – take waterproofs, plenty of food and drink and basic tools – especially spare inner tubes and tyre repair equipment. Tell someone where you are going and approximately when you are due back. You are more likely to tumble off your bike riding off-road, so you should consider wearing a helmet and mittens with padded palms.

Local Tourist Information Centres

Coldstream
Town Hall, High Street, Coldstream
Telephone (01890) 882607

Dunbar
143 High Street, Dunbar
Telephone (01368) 863353

Edinburgh
3 Princes Street, Edinburgh
Telephone 0131 473 3800

Eyemouth
Auld Kirk, Market Place, Eyemouth
Telephone (01890) 750678

Galashiels
3 St John Street, Galashiels
Telephone (01896) 755551

Hawick
Drumlanrig's Tower, Tower Knowe, Hawick
Telephone (01450) 372547

Jedburgh
Murray's Green, Jedburgh
Telephone (01835) 863435

Kelso
Town House, The Square, Kelso
Telephone (01573) 223464

Linlithgow
Burgh Halls, The Cross, Linlithgow
Telephone (01506) 844600

Melrose
Abbey House, Abbey Street, Melrose
Telephone (01896) 822555

Musselburgh
Old Craighall, By Musselburgh
Telephone 0131 653 6172

North Berwick
1 Quality Street, North Berwick
Telephone (01620) 892197

Peebles
High Street, Peebles
Telephone (01721) 720138

Selkirk
Halliwells House, Selkirk
Telephone (01750) 20054

Local cycle hire

Bikesport, Peebles Road, Innerleithen
Telephone (01896) 830880

Central Cycle Hire
13 Lochrin Place, Edinburgh
Telephone (0131 228 6333

Crossburn Caravans Cycle Hire
Edinburgh Road, Peebles
Telephone (01721) 720501

Edinburgh Cycle Hire
29 Blackfriars Street, Edinburgh
Telephone 0131 556 5560

Gala Cycles
38 Island Street, Galashiels
Telephone (01896) 75787

Great Bikes
25-27 Iona Street, Leith, Edinburgh
Telephone 0131 467 7775

Hawick Cycle Centre
Mart Street, Hawick
Telephone (01450) 373352

Scottish Border Trails
Drummore, Venlaw High Road, Peebles
Telephone (01721) 720336

Local cycle shops

Gala Cycles, Hawick Cycle Centre, Bikesport.

Bathgate Bikes
21 King Street, Bathgate
Telephone (01506) 632727

The Bike Shed
1D Tait Street, Dalkeith
Telephone 0131 654 1170

P & S Dorricot
53 High Street, Jedburgh
Telephone (01835) 862423

Free Wheelin
26 Edinburgh Road, Penicuik
Telephone (01968) 673127

Henderson Outdoor Leisure
Mayfield Garden Centre, Kelso
Telephone (01573) 228200

George Pennel Cycles
3 High Street, Peebles
Telephone (01721) 720844

COLINTON, BALERNO AND THE PENTLANDS

Route information

Distance   20km (12.5 miles)

Grade   Moderate

Terrain   Minor roads and firm off-road tracks, suitable for all bicycles. Much of the route is level, with one climb out of Balerno and a long descent back into Colinton. Note that you may have to lift your bike over one gate.

Time to allow   2 hours.

Getting there by car   Colinton is 7km (4.5 miles) south west of the centre of Edinburgh and can be reached via the A70 and B701. There is car parking at Old Colinton Station, under Colinton Bridge (Bridge Road).

Getting there by train   Kingsknowe Station is just over 2.5km (1.5 miles) from the start of the route at Colinton Bridge. TL out of the station, into Kingsknowe Road South. At top, TR on to Lanark Road. TL at Gillespie XR into Gillespie Road and descend to Colinton Bridge. TL onto track just before bridge. Telephone (0345) 484950 for timetable information.

The route begins in Colinton, in the wooded valley of the Water of Leith, and follows a disused railway track as far as Balerno. It then climbs into the foothills of the Pentlands to visit first a wildlife reserve and then a series of reservoirs, linked by tracks and minor roads. Exhilarating descents take you back to Colinton.

Route description

Start on the Water of Leith Walkway, under Colinton Bridge (Bridge Road) and head south west, SP Balerno. After 200m, pass gateway on left into Spylaw Park. Continue as track becomes a road and cross the Water of Leith. As road bends left, continue SO on track.

1   Continue on track as it passes under city bypass, crosses Grain Mill Road. At Juniper Green station, follow track, as it veers right at end of station leaving tarmac (where stone wall begins on left). After 500m, pass old Kinleith Mill, now mostly derelict. After a further 300m, the track crosses a heavily wooded stream, Poet's Glen.

2   Pass Currie Kirk on left and continue on track.   ***3.5km (2 miles)***

3   The track ends at Bridge Road in Balerno. TL into Bridge Road (5.5km/3.5 miles). To visit Malleny Garden, TL into Bavelaw Road and follow SP Malleny Garden; retrace and TL into Bridge Road. Continue SO to roundabout and TL, SP Deanpark.

4   After 30m, as road goes right, continue SO into cobbled Main Street. Continue onto path at top of street, leading to Mansfield Road. Continue SO for a steady climb with views of Black Hill ahead. After derestriction SP, road enters countryside and an avenue of trees. The road levels and then climbs again, past Animal Welfare Centre.

5   Bear left at top of hill, SP Red Moss Wildlife Reserve. Continue past car park to information board and gateway. SO here for 200m to a bridge to view Bavelaw Marsh on right, Threipmuir Reservoir on left (9km/ 5.5 miles). Retrace to information board and either lift bike over gate to orange track, or retrace to car park and TR (the two tracks meet at SP To the Hills). Continue.

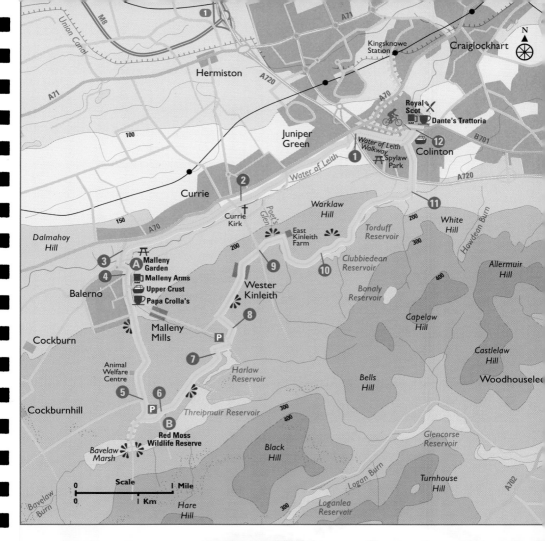

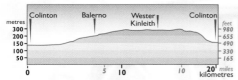

TL onto track at metal footbridge onto track and continue past Harlaw Reservoir.

7 Lift bike over gate if it is locked and continue on track. **12km (7.5 miles)**

8 TL at TJ, no SP, passing car park and information board on left. TR at TJ, no SP (opposite farm). Views across Forth valley to Ochil Hills, West Lothian and the Trossachs. As road descends, it turns sharp right at farm cottages (Wester Kinleith) – take care.

6 SO through gate. Views of Threipmuir Reservoir, and East and West Kip – two of the highest hills in the Pentlands. At second gate, follow track round to right. Arrive east end of Threipmuir Reservoir (use path if cobbles wet).

9 SO at XR, no SP (white house, Mid Kinleith, on right). Views of west Edinburgh, Forth Bridges, Fife and the estuary. Continue descent, crossing Poet's Glen again. Then slight uphill to East Kinleith Farm, where TR (sharply) onto track, keeping cottages on left and information board on right.

10 Continue, passing Clubbiedean Reservoir. At east end, track becomes tarmac for short while and descends steeply – there is a sharp bend at foot of hill and gravel – take care (16km/10 miles). Continue steep descent (on tarmac), passing Torduff Reservoir. Views of Arthur's Seat and Salisbury Crags.

11 TL at TJ, no SP, and cross city bypass. Continue long descent down Bonaly Road and at foot of hill, TR into Woodhall Road, no SP.

12 TL (sharply) at traffic lights, into Bridge Road. Continue through village to Colinton Bridge. TR onto track at west end of bridge and return to Old Colinton Station and the end of the route. ***20km (12.5 miles)***

Places of interest along the route

En route, you pass a number of interesting places. Spylaw House and Park was built for James Gillespie, the snuffmaker, in 1773. The house has been converted into flats but the surrounding park, bordered by the Water of Leith, contains attractive trees, a children's play area and is a good spot for picnics. Poet's Glen is named for James Thomson, a contemporary of Burns, who lived at the head of the glen. The present Currie Kirk is around 200 years old, but there has been a church on this site for over 1000 years. The kirk and its neighbouring buildings make a pleasing composition much favoured by local artists.

Ⓐ Malleny Garden, Balerno
Walled garden dominated by four 400-year-old clipped yew trees. Also herbaceous borders,

Food and drink

Colinton and Balerno both have convenience stores.

Royal Scot, Colinton
Bar and restaurant meals. Conservatory at rear. Easy access from Water of Leith Walkway.

Dante's Trattoria, Colinton
Teas, coffees and ice cream.

Malleny Arms, Balerno
Food served all day.

Papa Crolla's Takeaway, Balerno
Pizzas, filled rolls and ice cream, served at lunchtime and in the evening. Closed Sunday.

a large collection of old-fashioned roses, Scotland's national bonsai collection and extensive woodland. Malleny House is closed to the public. National Trust for Scotland property. Open April to October, daily 0930–1900; November to March, daily 0930–1600. Charge. Telephone (01721) 722502 for further information.

Ⓑ Red Moss Wildlife Reserve
Red Moss Wildlife Reserve, managed by Scottish Wildlife, is a fine example of a raised bog – a series of hummocks and wet hollows sitting over 3m (12 feet) of water, supporting a variety of plants and animals. Bavelaw Marsh and adjacent Threipmuir Reservoir are home to a great variety of birds, migrants and residents, and other wildlife. There are several information boards on site; nature notes (and information on cycling in the area) are available from the Ranger Centre at the end of Harlaw Reservoir. Open at all reasonable times. Admission free. For further information, telephone the Ranger Centre on (0131 449 5816).

NORTH EDINBURGH – CRAMOND AND THE WATER OF LEITH

Route information

Distance   22.5km (14 miles)

Grade   Easy

Terrain   Undulating, off-road tracks following disused railway tracks and cycleways, mostly tarmacked. There are two flights of steps to be negotiated towards the end of the route.

Time to allow   2–3 hours.

Getting there by car   Wester Coates Terrace, Roseburn is 2km (1 mile) west of Edinburgh's West End on the Glasgow Road (A8). From the city, TR into Wester Coates Terrace just before the brightly-painted old railway bridge. You can park in this residential street.

Getting there by train   The nearest station is Edinburgh Haymarket. From the station, TL into Haymarket Terrace and continue SO to old railway bridge (use bus lane). TL at filling station for 20m and TR up path, keeping right to cross bridge and access the track at the start of the route.

Edinburgh's extensive network of suburban railway has now been largely converted to cycle/walkway and the surfaces tarmacked. This route explores a number of these tracks and the Esplanade which runs along the foreshore from Cramond to Granton. The return route follows the Water of Leith track, through Dean Village.

Places of interest along the route

Ⓐ Lauriston Castle

Lauriston Castle gives visitors a snapshot of the interior of a Scottish Edwardian country house. The house itself is a 16th-century tower house, extensively enlarged during the 19th century. The last private owners were the Reid family, proprietors of a prestigious Edinburgh firm of cabinet makers and house furnishers. The house contains William Reid's fine collection of period and reproduction furniture, Derbyshire Blue John ornaments and objets d'art. In 1926 the house was left to the nation and has since been administered by the City of Edinburgh. Tearoom. Grounds open all year, daily dawn–dusk. Castle (each visitor is given a guided tour lasting approximately 40 minutes) open April to October, Saturday–Thursday 1100–1300 and 1400–1700; November to March, Saturday and Sunday 1400–1600. Charge. Telephone 0131 336 2060.

Ⓑ Cramond

Cramond, on the River Almond, is an attractive 18th-century village, restored in the 1960s. The Romans built a harbour here. The kirk was constructed during the 15th and 16th century. Cramond Tower, now a private residence, was originally built as a summer palace for the medieval Bishops of Dunkeld. During the 18th and 19th centuries iron works were established along the River Almond – the first commercially produced Scottish crude steel came from Cramond.

🔵 St Bernard's Well, Water of Leith

The building surrounding this mineral spring was designed by Alexander Nasmyth for Lord Gardenstone in 1788. It comprises ten Doric columns and a statue of Hygeia, Goddess of Health. At one time the public could pay a fee of 1d per day to sample the waters, and the custodian required customers to 'walk about, or take other exercise for at least five minutes afterwards'.

🔵 Dean Village

Dean Bridge was built by Thomas Telford in 1832 to carry the main road from Edinburgh to Queensferry. The village was the abode of baxters (bakers) and millers – during the 17th century there were 11 mills in the village. Various buildings have sculptured panels commemorating the baxters. One panel passed en route reads 'God bless the Baxters of Edinburgh who built this Hous 1675' and shows crossed peels, the implements used to pull loaves from the ovens.

🔵 Scottish National Gallery of Modern Art

Housed in a building designed in the 1820s, formerly a school, the gallery has almost 4000 works of art – mostly amassed since the 1960s. The collection includes sculptures by Barbara Hepworth, Eduardo Paolozzi, Henry Moore and others, and 20th-century Scottish art. Restaurant and gift shop. Open all year, Monday–Saturday 1000–1700, Sunday 1400–1700. Admission free. Telephone 0131 624 6332.

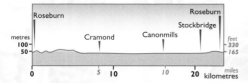

Route description

The route starts on a traffic-free track. If you have arrived by car, access to the track is from Wester Coates Terrace, opposite Wester Coates Avenue, no SP. TR onto main track (take care – blind junction) and cross viaduct over Water of Leith. Follow track as it enters cutting. At old Craigleith Station, track goes under Queensferry Road.

1 LHF at junction of tracks, no SP but opposite Sainsbury's and Craigleith Retail Park (1.5km/1 mile). After 300m, pass under Telford Road and continue on track as it climbs quite steeply.

2 LHF at junction of tracks, and continue under bridge, SP Cramond Brig, onto dust track, which ends in supermarket car park. Cross car park and exit to main road (Cramond Road South). TL to visit Davidson's Mains. Otherwise, TR for 200m. To visit Lauriston Castle continue for further 100m. To continue route, TR into Lauriston Farm Road.

3 TL at roundabout into Silverknowes Road and continue.

4 SO at roundabout, across pavement, past barrier on left and down ramp to Esplanade. TL, by tearoom, and cycle along Esplanade to Cramond, taking care as the area is popular with walkers (5.5km/3.5 miles). Visit Cramond and return along Esplanade, keeping SO at tearoom.

5 Near end of Esplanade (after rugby posts), TL down track towards sea, no SP. TR along seafront, keeping industrial area on right. Pass barrier onto West Shore Road where TR for 50m. TL through barrier onto tarmac track, at SP Bruce Glaziers Haulage. *11.5km (7 miles)*

6 Pass another barrier and TR at Caroline Park (18th-century house, used as offices). Continue on minor road, gasworks on right, for 200m. Before bridge over old railway, TL down track and go through barrier, no SP. TR at foot of track onto old railway track, the Pilton Path. Continue.

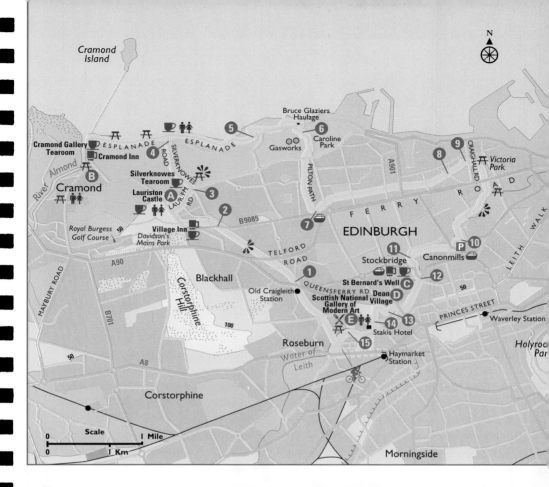

7 TL at TJ of tracks, before bridge over Ferry Road, no SP. Continue.

8 SO at five-way junction of tracks, SP Victoria Park. **15.5km (9.5 miles)**

9 TR at TJ of tracks, SP Victoria Park. Cycle under Craighall Road and into Victoria Park. TL at TJ of paths in park, SP Stedfastgate. Cycle under Ferry Road. Views of Calton Hill, Salisbury Crags and Arthur's Seat. RHF at XR of paths (Stedfastgate), SP Warriston along Old Railway. Continue on this track.

10 At start of supermarket car park, TR through barrier into residential road. Cycle to end of road where TL and walk (against one-

way) 100m to Canonmills (18km/11 miles). TR over bridge. TL after 100m, into Inverleith Terrace Lane, SP Water of Leith Walkway (cobbled surface). Continue onto Rocheid Path, beside Water of Leith.

11 TL at end of Rocheid Path, into Arboretum Avenue. TR at TJ into St Bernard's Row (cobbled surface). TL at TJ (traffic lights) and into Stockbridge.

12 TR at second set of lights (XR), into Saunders Street (19.5km/12 miles). Cycle under archway at end of street and TL up steps. Pass St Bernard's Well on right. Continue to Dean Village.

Cramond Inn

13 Track ends at Dean Village. TR and cross Water of Leith. TL into Damside for 50m. TL again (cobbled surface), small SP Damside Nos 1-4. Go carefully past barrier and down steep slope to very edge of water where TR. Go up steps beside weir and follow track through woods – watch out for pedestrians.

14 TL at Belford Bridge, to go under bridge and past Hilton Hotel. Cross river via footbridge. Continue on track for 1km (0.6mile).

15 To visit Gallery of Modern Art TR and follow track over footbridge (long flight of steps to gallery). Otherwise continue beside Water of Leith. Cycle under viaduct (which carries railway path we started on). Track ends at flight of steps. Go up these, TR and then TL at main road for 100m, past lights. TL into Wester Coates Terrace to complete the route.

22.5km (14 miles)

Food and drink

There are pubs and a bakery and tea-room in Davidson's Mains, a sandwich shop, bakery and sweet shop in Canon-mills, and a variety of eateries in Stock-bridge. Lauriston Castle and the Gallery of Modern Art offer refreshments.

Village Inn, Davidson's Mains
Close to the route. Food served all day.

Silverknowes Tearoom, Silverknowes
On the Esplanade, between Granton and Cramond. Open weekends in summer.

Cramond Gallery Tearoom, Cramond
Beside the ferry and boat harbour.

Cramond Inn, Cramond
Food served all day.

Route information

Distance 24km (15 miles)

Grade Easy

Terrain Gently undulating, mostly quiet lanes.

Time to allow 2–3 hours.

Getting there by car Tranent is 18km (11 miles) east of Edinburgh, 2km (1 mile) off the A1 (signed). There is a car park behind the High Street at the Loch Centre, Loch Road (turn off the B6371/Ormiston Road).

Getting there by train The nearest railway station is Prestonpans. From the station, TL and TL again, to pass under railway. Follow cycle SP for Tranent, 2.5km (1.5 mile) away. Civic Square is in the High Street.

From Tranent, through New Winton, a model estate village built in the early 19th century, and on past Winton House, a Jacobean mansion built in 1620. The route continues through Pencaitland and West and East Saltoun, before returning to Tranent.

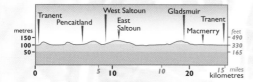

Places of interest along the route

West Saltoun contains a fine church and fountain and, as you pass through the village, an information board on the left gives local history notes.

A Tranent

The mining town of Tranent is known for the massacre of 1797, when the Militia Act was imposed to raise troops to supplement the regular army. The miners of Tranent resisted the military recruitment and then clashed with the troops sent to restore order. Twelve local men were killed and many others wounded. In 1997 a bronze statue was erected to commemorate Jackie Crookston, one of the men killed.

B Pencaitland

Divided by the Tyne Water, Pencaitland has a fine three-arched bridge, dating from 1510. The village contains many picturesque buildings, including the Caledonian Arms, an old coach stop with stables at the rear, Hope Cottage with a grand wrought-iron gateway and The Old Smiddy, now a pub and restaurant. The war memorial was designed by Robert Lorimer, a famous domestic architect. A board by the church gives information on places of interest in the village. The tiny pan-tiled house at the church entrance is where the church elders sat, to take the collection from the parishioners.

Route description

The start of the route is Civic Square. From the car park, follow the pedestrian link from the Loch Centre to the High Street via Plough Lane and TL for Civic Square. From Civic Square, head east along High Street and TR, SP Ormiston/B6371 for 1km (0.6 mile). LHF at junction onto B6355, SP Pencaitland. Continue on B6355, until you are 1km (0.6 mile) beyond New Winton.

1 As road bends left, SO through ornamental archway (entrance to Winton Estate). Look out for road humps and a cattle grid. Continue SO past Winton House, keeping on main route to exit park through another gateway, into Pencaitland and junction with A6093.

2 TR onto A6093 (6km/3.5 miles). Note information board on church wall on left. Cross bridge with traffic lights, over Tyne Water.

3 TL at TJ, SP Lempock Wells.

4 TL at XR, SP West Saltoun, and cross Burns Water. Continue SO at all junctions, through West Saltoun to East Saltoun.

5 In East Saltoun, TL at fountain, no SP, for 50m. TR into small road, no SP but by three-storey stone house (11km/7 miles). Continue on this road. TL at TJ at grassy triangle, no SP.

6 TR (effectively SO) at TJ (grassy triangle), no SP. Then, TL at TJ at Begbie Farm, no SP. Continue for 300m.

7 TL (effectively SO) at TJ, over bridge and through hamlet of Samuelston.

8 SO at XR, SP Gladsmuir.   *16km (10 miles)*

9 TL at TJ. Continue and as road goes right, go SO on minor road which becomes narrow and winding, to arrive at Gladsmuir.

10 TL at TJ. This is the old A1, with little traffic and cycle lanes (19km/12 miles). Continue SO through all junctions, through Macmerry to Tranent and the end of the route.

24km (15 miles)

Food and drink

There are convenience stores in Pencaitland, East Saltoun and Macmerry.

Ken's Open Oven, Tranent
Filled rolls, sandwiches, soup, tea and coffee.

Caledonian Arms, Pencaitland
Morning coffee and bar lunches available.

The Old Smiddy, Pencaitland
Pub and restaurant in the old blacksmith's shop.

Farmland, East Lothian

THE TWEED VALLEY – MELROSE TO DRYBURGH

Route information

Distance 24.5km (15 miles)

Grade Moderate

Terrain Quite a hilly ride with climbs on both sides of the Tweed, including one over the shoulder of the Eildon Hills, with an exhilarating, long descent back to Darnick and Melrose. Mostly minor roads with little traffic, following the Tweed Cycleway between Melrose and Dryburgh.

Time to allow 2–3 hours.

Getting there by car Melrose is 56km (35 miles) south of Edinburgh, reached via the A68 and A6091. From town centre head down Abbey Street, and the car park is on the left, opposite Melrose Abbey.

Getting there by train There is no rail service to Melrose, but some buses from Edinburgh will take bikes. Telephone Lowland Buses for further information on 0131 663 1945.

This route takes advantage of the Tweed Cycleway and visits two of the four famous Borders Abbeys – Melrose and Dryburgh – as well as Scott's View, the Leaderfoot Viaduct and the Wallace Statue. This is a short route, but allow plenty of time to enjoy the sights and the magnificent scenery of this part of the Tweed valley.

Route description

TL out of the car park opposite Melrose Abbey and head down Abbey Street, keeping the abbey on your right. Continue as road bends right, following SP Tweed Cycleway, all the way into Newstead, where the road climbs quite sharply.

1 TL by a small green, just before meeting main road, and go around a steel gate. Continue. Pass the site of the Roman fort Trimontium. Descend to foot of hill, with view of Leaderfoot Viaduct ahead.

2 TL, SP Tweed Cycleway. Cross old bridge over River Tweed and TR at end of bridge, SP Tweed Cycleway. Pass under main road and SO at TJ, SP Scott's View. Cross Leader Water for steep climb.

3 TR at TJ onto minor road, SP Tweed Cycleway. View back of viaduct and Eildon Hills. Continue climbing. SO at TJ, SP Scott's View. Pass Scott's View (6.5km/4 miles) and descend steeply. Take care on left hand bend. Continue and pass SP Wallace Statue. The statue is a 300m walk through wood. Take bike, or lock it at gate. Continue route with steep descent (1:11).

4 TR at TJ, SP Dryburgh Abbey and continue to Dryburgh. To visit the abbey, continue SO for 300m. To continue route, TR at TJ, SP Melrose/No Exit (9.5km/6 miles). Descend to riverside and continue to end of road. Cross footbridge over River Tweed. Continue, climbing out of valley with views back of Abbey.

5 SO at staggered XR with A68 (use the central reservation when crossing), SP Newtown St Boswells. TL at TJ, SP Whitelee (or SO for Dryburgh Arms Hotel). Take care at

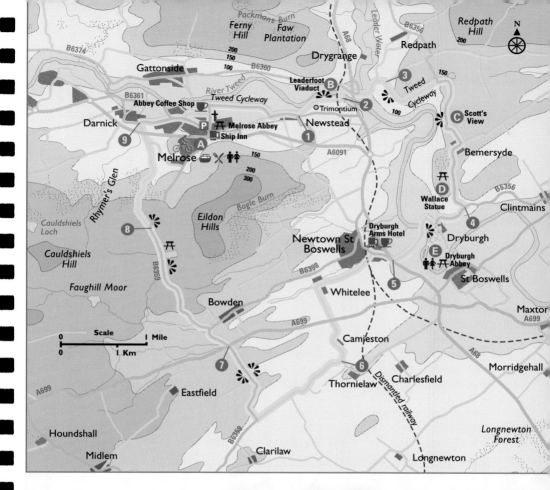

double bend under former railway line. Follow road as bends left in Whitelee. Climb and SO at XR, SP Charlesfield.

6 TR at TJ, SP Lilliesleaf. Continue. TR at TJ, SP Melrose (16km/10 miles) and climb again. Views south and east at summit. Descend.

7 SO at XR for 300m, SP Melrose. Then, TL (effectively) SO at TJ, SP Melrose, for a long steady climb. Picturesque loch-side picnic spot at summit. ***20.5km (12.5 miles)***

8 SO onto minor road, no SP (where main road bears right, SP Melrose). Views to north and east. Continue on long descent through woods, steep in parts. At foot of hill, bear left at TJ, no SP. SO under A6091.

9 TR at TJ, no SP. Then, TR at TJ, SP Newtown St Boswells. Continue and TL at TJ, SP Newstead B6361. The end of the route and the car park are on left after 200m. ***24.5km (15 miles)***

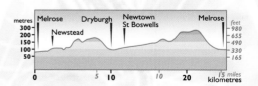

Places of interest along the route

A Melrose

Melrose Abbey, now a ruin in the town square, was founded by David I circa 1136. On the roof of the abbey is a carving of a pig playing the bagpipes. Historic Scotland property. Gift shop and picnic area. Open April to September, Monday–Saturday 0930–1830, Sunday 1400–1830; October to March, Monday–Saturday 0930–1830, Sunday 1400–1630. Charge. Telephone (01896) 822562. **Priorwood Garden and Dried Flower Shop**, by the abbey, is a unique garden specialising in plants suitable for drying. National Trust for Scotland property. Gift shop. Open April to September, Monday–Saturday 1000–1730, Sunday 1330–1730; October to December, Monday–Saturday 1000–1600, Sunday 1330–1600. Charge. Telephone (01896) 822493. **Harmony Garden**, opposite the abbey and also a National Trust for Scotland property, contains spring bulbs, herbaceous and mixed borders, and fruiting apricots. Open Easter to September, Monday–Saturday 1000–1730, Sunday 1330–1730. Charge. Telephone (01721) 722502. The **Teddy Melrose Teddy Bear Museum**, in the town square, houses fascinating displays recording the heritage of British teddy bears. Gift shop, tearoom and garden picnic area. Open all year, daily 1000–1700. Charge. Telephone (01896) 822464. **Trimontium**, in the town square, is an award-winning exhibition illustrating daily life on the Roman frontier. Gift shop. Open April–October, daily 1030–1630. Charge. Telephone (01896) 822651.

B Leaderfoot Viaduct, near Melrose

The viaduct was built in 1865 to carry the Berwickshire Railway from Newtown St Boswells to Earlston and Duns. It has 19 arches and stands 40m (123 feet) tall. Passenger traffic ceased in 1948 and the line was finally closed in 1965. The viaduct is now being restored. Access at all reasonable times. Free. For further information, telephone Melrose Tourist Information Centre on (01896) 822555.

C Scott's View, near Melrose

A view (at 181m/593 feet above sea level) over the Tweed valley to the Eildon Hills, beloved by Scott. An information board names various points of interest. Access at all reasonable times. Free. For further information, telephone Melrose Tourist Information Centre, number above.

D Wallace Statue, near Dryburgh

A massive sandstone statue, erected in 1814 by David Stuart Erskine, Earl of Buchan, situated in woodland overlooking the river and surrounding countryside. Close by, a vase of similar proportions, mounted on a plinth of natural rock, bears a lengthy inscription about William Wallace. Good picnic spot. Access at all reasonable times. Free. For further information, telephone Melrose Tourist Information Centre, number above.

E Dryburgh Abbey, near Dryburgh

The remarkably complete ruins of another of the abbeys founded by David I. Gift shop and picnic area. Historic Scotland property. Open April to September, Monday–Saturday 0930–1830, Sunday 1400–1830; October to March, Monday–Saturday 0930–1830, Sunday 1400–1630. Charge. Telephone (01835) 822381.

Food and drink

There are plenty of opportunities for refreshment in Melrose, including a tearoom at the Teddy Bear Museum.

Abbey Coffee Shop, Melrose
Coffees, teas and lunches served.

Ship Inn, Melrose
Bar meals offered.

Dryburgh Arms Hotel, Newtown St Boswells
Close to the route, serving morning coffee and snacks.

Route information

Distance 25km (15.5 miles)

Grade Moderate

Terrain Some quite long (but not too severe) hills, with swooping descents. Mostly minor roads but an unavoidable 1km (0.6 mile) along the A68. Two short off-road sections suitable for most types of bicycle.

Time to allow 2–3 hours.

Getting there by car Lauder is 40km (25 miles) south of Edinburgh on the A68. Park in Market Square in the town centre.

Getting there by train There are no rail services to Lauder but some buses from Edinburgh will carry bicycles. For further information, telephone Lowland Buses on 0131 663 1945.

This route is through the beautiful, wooded countryside of the Scottish Borders. There are extensive views of Lauderdale and the Eildon Hills throughout. The Roman road followed along the valley is the historic Dere Street, which linked Cramond, near Edinburgh, to York via Jedburgh.

Places of interest along the route

A Lauder

The town of Lauder dates back to the 12th century. It received a Royal Charter in 1502 – the Scottish parliament met in the town many times. Close to the border, Lauder was involved in every border war. Today the town is designated an Outstanding Conservation Area and retains its 14th-century Tolbooth, opposite the 17th-century kirk which is built in the shape of a Greek cross. For further information, telephone Jedburgh Tourist Information Centre on (01835) 863435. **Thirlestane Castle**, on the outskirts of Lauder, was originally built as a defensive fort in the 13th century. It was rebuilt by the Maitland family during the 16th century. Visitors can tour the house. Also woodland walks, picnic area, tearoom and giftshop. Open Easter, May, June and September, Monday, Wednesday, Thursday and Sunday 1400–1700; July and August, Sunday–Friday 1200–1700. Charge. Telephone (01578) 722430.

B Earlston

Earlston sits on the east bank of the Leader Water and is where David I signed the charter for the founding of Melrose Abbey. The town is traditionally supposed to be the birthplace of Thomas Rhymer, poet and prophet (it was said that he could never lie), circa 1220. A stone in the east wall of the church commemorates this and Rhymer's Tower, now a ruin, lies behind the café and petrol station on the main road.

Food and drink

Lauder and Earlston have pubs, tea-rooms and convenience stores. Refreshments are available at Thirlestane Castle.

☕ **Flat Cat Gallery, Lauder**
Open seven days a week, offering light meals and cakes.

☕ **Leader Café, Earlston**
Traditional café with home baking.

☕ **Rhymer's Tower Coffee Shop, Earlston**
Serves breakfast, lunch, home baking and take-aways.

Route description

Start in Lauder's Market Square and head south on the A68 – take care as this road can be busy. Pass lodge and entrance to Thirlestane Castle on left, SP Southern Upland Way. Continue on A68.

1 TR at TJ onto the Roman road, SP Blainslie, for a steady climb. Continue on road as it descends through Nether Blainslie, and continue SO at all junctions as the undulating road crosses streams, tributaries of the Leader Water from the hills on the right.

2 TL at Clackmae Farm, into farm road, SP Leadervale/No Exit (9 km/5.5 miles). SO onto track at entrance to Leadervale House (woods on left, stone wall on right). Descend steeply. Cross the Leader Water via footbridge. LHF at TJ by farm-house, and continue along valley into Earlston.

Thirlestane Castle

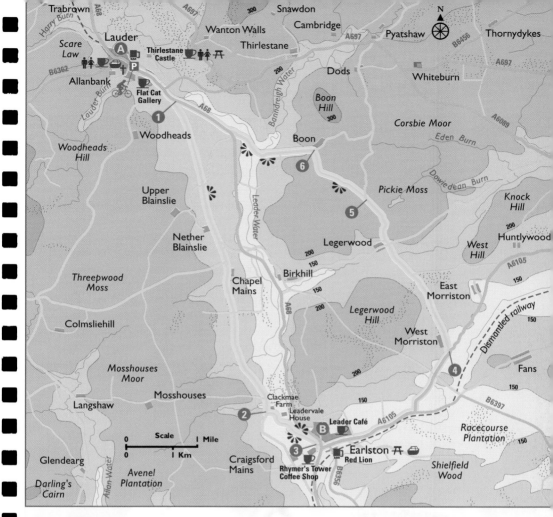

3 TL onto slip road for 10 metres. Then TR onto A68 and almost immediately TL into High Street, SP Town Centre (10.5km/6.5 miles). Continue through Earlston and after 2.5km (1.5 miles) TL (effectively SO) at TJ, SP Berwick A6105.

4 At West Morriston TL at TJ, SP Legerwood, for a steady climb, then descent to Legerwood. SO at XR, SP Boon, for another climb (17.5km/ 11 miles). Continue for 1km (0.6 mile) uphill, between avenue of trees.

5 LHF onto track, no SP (but before road bends to right). Track climbs, then descends, steeply in places. Views of Lauderdale.

6 TL at end of track (in Boon, by white house), onto minor road. Follow road down to the Leader Water and cross via Bailey-type bridge. Views back of Eildon Hills. TR at TJ onto A68, no SP, and follow road back into Lauder to complete the route. **25km (15.5 miles)**

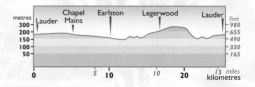

HOLYROOD PARK, MUSSELBURGH AND PORTOBELLO

Route information

Distance 25km (15.5 miles)

Grade Easy

Terrain Gently undulating minor roads and well-surfaced off-road tracks. Two short sections of main road (which can be walked), and one climb towards the end of the route.

Time to allow 3 hours.

Getting there by car The start of the route, the Commonwealth Pool car park, is in Holyrood Park Road, off St Leonard's Street/Dalkeith Road (A7) in Newington, Edinburgh.

Getting there by train The nearest railway station is Edinburgh Waverley, 2km (1 mile) from the start of the route. TL out of the station (south side). TL at mini roundabout into East Market Street, bear right into Jeffrey Street, and continue SO (along The Pleasance and St Leonard's Street). The Commonwealth Pool is on the left.

This route mostly uses off-road tracks within Edinburgh. From the Commonwealth Pool by Holyrood Park, the route follows a disused railway track around the dominating hill of Arthur's Seat, along the River Esk into Musselburgh and on to Fisherrow, a small, pleasant harbour with fishing boats. The route continues through the seaside town of Portobello before returning via the northern side of Holyrood Park.

Places of interest along the route

🅐 Innocent Railway, Edinburgh

This was the first railway into Edinburgh, completed in 1831. The wagons were pulled by horses. The name Innocent came from the fact that, in comparison with the more sophisticated railways using steam locomotives, accidents on this railway line were less severe. The passenger service ended in 1860 but goods traffic continued until 1968. A section of the line has been converted to traffic-free track, for cyclists and pedestrians. Access at all reasonable times. Free. For further information, contact the Tourist Information Centre in Musselburgh on 0131 653 6172.

🅑 Portobello

The seaside town of Portobello attracts large numbers of day visitors. The seafront boasts refurbished Victorian Baths and a Fun Park, and there are lots of places to eat and drink. The beach is a lovely stretch of golden sand with breakwaters, and views along the coast of East Lothian. Telephone Musselburgh Tourist Information Centre (telephone number above) for further information.

🅒 Holyrood Park, Edinburgh

There has probably been a Royal Park here since the Augustinian Abbey was founded in the early 12th century. The park was formally enclosed in 1541, during the reign of James V. It includes Arthur's Seat and there are several romantic ruins as well as archaeological sites. History Scotland property. Open at all reasonable times. Admission free. The **Palace of**

Holyroodhouse is the official residence of the Queen in Scotland. Both properties run by Historic Scotland. Gift shop. Open at all times, except before, during and after Royal and State visits. April to October, Monday–Saturday 0930–1715, Sunday 1030–1630; November to March, Monday–Saturday 0930–1545. Charge. Telephone 0131 556 7371. **Holyrood Abbey** is in the grounds of the Palace of Holyroodhouse and comprises the ruined nave of the 12th- and 13th-century Augustinian Abbey. **Dynamic Earth**, Holyrood Road, describes the story of Earth through dramatic special effects and interactive displays. Restaurant, bar and picnic area. Open April to October, daily 1000–1800; November to March, Wednesday–Sunday 1000–1700. Charge. Telephone 0131 550 7800. Holyrood is also the location of the new Scottish parliament.

Food and drink

There is a cafeteria at the Commonwealth Pool and plenty of opportunities for refreshment in Musselburgh and Portobello. The church in Bellfield Street, Portobello, serves tea, coffee, filled rolls and home baking on weekdays, 1000–1400. There is usually a mobile hot food snack bar at Fisherrow.

Harbour Shop, Fisherrow
Snacks and filled rolls.

Engine Shed, St Leonard's
Employment centre for handicapped young people, including café and bakery.

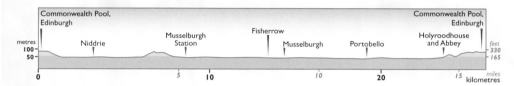

Palace of Holyroodhouse

Route description

TR out of car park, towards Salisbury Crags. Take first TL, into East Parkside (blue SP). At first opening, TR and TR again, under footbridge and past garages. The tunnel visible ahead marks the start of the Innocent Railway and descends on gradient of 1:30. View, from tunnel, of Arthur's Seat at close quarters, and Duddingston Kirk in distance. Continue on track – it is wooded and sheltered by walls, but care is required as the surface is broken by tree roots.

1 SO as track crosses Duddingston Road West, SP Bingham.

2 SO at XR of tracks, SP The Jewel. Continue on track as it bends left and is joined by Brunstane Burn. Track crosses Duddingston Park South, where SO, SP Brunstane, keeping burn on right.

3 Just before main road bridge, TR (sharply) on track (doubling back on yourself). Cross burn and exit into The Jewel (road name), opposite supermarket. Cross road where SP No Vehicles Except Buses and make for orange track behind and to right of supermarket (5km/ 3 miles). Cross two railway lines and TL through gateway onto tarred track. Exit into service road, keeping right into (Kinnaird Retail Park).

4 After road bends left, TR onto track, SP Bus Stop. Exit to main road and TR for 50m. TL at roundabout, and again TL, SP Fisherrow. At foot of hill TR at TJ and climb. Continue on road and cross railway and another bridge, over waste ground.

5 TL through barrier, SP Fisherrow. Cycle under A1 road and TR at TJ of tracks. Pass another barrier and follow road as it goes left (old Mucklets Road).

6 Arrive Musselburgh Station and TR onto cycle track, SP Monktonhall.

8.5km (5 miles)

7 After first railway bridge TL at TJ of tracks, and follow track between railway and field. Cycle under second railway bridge and

exit to residential road. Continue for 30m, then TL for another 30m and TR. SO at roundabout, SP No Exit Except Cycles. Continue, as residential road becomes minor road, goes under railway and becomes track, crossing River Esk via footbridge.

8 TL, at TJ of tracks, no SP (10km/6 miles). Continue on track, under railway, following River Esk, past Inveresk and into Musselburgh, where track exits onto service road (Station Road).

9 As road starts to leave river (opposite distinctive building with round tower and turret) get on pavement and turn hard L up to main road, cross it and continue on track beside river.

10 Stay on track as it dips under main road, passing old stone fountain on right. Note High Street on right, for shops and cafés (13km/ 8 miles). Continue beside river until last bridge (footbridge), where TL across it.

11 SO, along New Street, passing Fisherrow on right after 1km (0.6 mile). Continue SO, to main road (Edinburgh Road) where TR for 500m (busy road – walk along pavement if necessary). TL at traffic light junction for 30m, SP City Centre.

12 TL onto gravel track, no SP but opposite motor garage (15.5km/9.5 miles). Stay on track – it crosses Brunstane Burn and bears right up hill; then goes left at fence and climbs steeply, following line of fence; under railway, across burn and along right bank for short climb. Track exits to minor road through hole in wall, where TR for 40m. TR again, into Brunstane Road South, and continue to junction with Milton Road East.

13 At main road, go onto pavement (shared use). TL, then bear right through underpass, bear left up ramp and TL at top (still on pavement). TL again, into Magdalene Drive, SP 20 Zone.

14 TR into Magdalene Avenue. After 200m TR onto track (opposite Magdalene Place) to main road, where SO (use crossing) into Hope Lane. Continue.

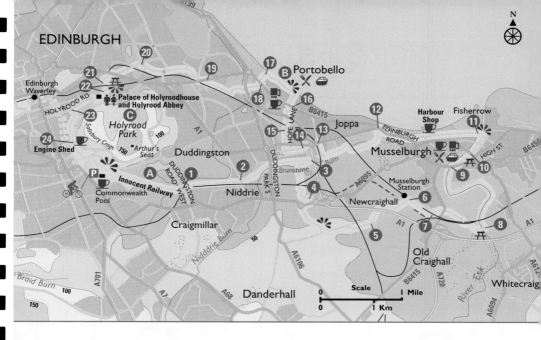

15 As lane bends left, continue SO, SP Portobello High Street. Cross railway and road, TL down ramp, SO at foot of ramp and cycle along St Marks Place. ***18.5km (11.5 miles)***

16 TL at TJ, into High Street. Then TR into Bellfield Street. Continue to seafront, where TL along Promenade. Cycle with care – there may be pedestrians, children and dogs.

17 After Promenade does a double bend, TL into Westbank Street. Continue and TL into High Street.

18 TR into Fishwives Causeway. SO at roundabout, use light-controlled crossing across bypass, and continue along Fishwives Causeway. Continue SO (as road turns right) on track past single-pole barrier, to back lane beside railway. Continue.

19 TL into Moira Terrace for 100m. TR, before bridge, and immediately TL into Restalrig Avenue. SO at roundabout, into Marionville Avenue. As road bends right, TL into Marionville Park, then TL at TJ into Marionville Road. ***22km (13.5 miles)***

20 TL at roundabout, then TR at lights into London Road (busy road – walk along pavement if necessary). After 100m, TL into Abbey Lane.

21 TL at TJ, into Spring Gardens, then TR into Milton Street. At end of street TL into tiny passage for short flight of steps under arch dated 1693 and into Holyrood Park. TR at main path, towards Abbey. Pass tennis courts on left.

22 TL at TJ of tracks, keeping close to wall of Abbey on right. Keep right all way round Abbey wall, continue through car park, and exit onto road beside Palace. TL by gates and follow road round. SO at mini roundabout, into Holyrood Road for 600m.

23 TL, SP St John's Hill. TR into Viewcraig Gardens. At end of road, TL onto surfaced track. Continue and TR at TJ of tracks, into Braidwood Gate. Climb hill and follow track onto St Leonard's Hill.

24 Keep SO for 600m, passing Engine Shed. TR into Holyrood Park Road and Commonwealth Pool car park and end of route is on left. ***25km (15.5 miles)***

SOUTH QUEENSFERRY, HOPETOUN AND CRAMOND BRIG

Route information

 Distance   33.5km (21 miles)

Grade   Moderate

Terrain   Mostly level minor roads and off-road cycle tracks, with just one climb early on in the route. Suitable for all bicycles.

Time to allow   3 hours.

Getting there by car   South Queensferry is 18km (11 miles) north west of the centre of Edinburgh, off the A90 and near the Forth Road Bridge. Park in the Scotmid supermarket car park, off The Loan, the steep road leading down to the old part of the town.

Getting there by train   The nearest railway station is Dalmeny. TL out of the station for 800m. TR into Kirkliston Road, which becomes The Loan. Half-way down hill pass Queensferry Parish Church on the right and TL into Morison Gardens, no SP.

This route explores some popular areas for cycling on the north west side of Edinburgh, passing through woodland, farmland, parkland and along the seashore. Starting in South Queensferry, the route heads west to Hopetoun House, before turning east through Dalmeny, Cramond Brig and Davidsons Mains. The return passes close to the Forth Rail Bridge.

Places of interest along the route

A Hopetoun House, near South Queensferry
Hopetoun House features furniture, 17th-century tapestries, magnificent paintings and ceramics. The surrounding parkland contains gardens, a nature trail and several herds of deer. Marvellous views of the Forth Road and Rail Bridges. Gift shop, restaurant and picnic areas. Open Easter to September, daily 1000–1730. Charge. Telephone 0131 331 2451.

B Dalmeny Parish Church, Dalmeny
The best preserved Norman church in Scotland, dating from the 12th century. Gift shop. Open all year, Sunday 1400–1630 and at other times by request. Admission by donation. Telephone 0131 331 1479.

C Dalmeny House, Dalmeny
The home of the Earls of Rosebery for over 300 years, containing many works of art in splendid Gothic interiors. Tearoom. Open July and August, Monday and Tuesday 1200–1730, Sunday 1300–1730. Charge. Telephone 0131 331 1888.

D Cramond Brig, near Cramond
Bridge upstream from Cramond village, over the River Almond, believed to have been built around 1500 and rebuilt of stone in the 17th century. James V was attacked by thieves as he walked across the bridge. His rescuer, Jock Howison, was granted the adjacent land, Braehead, by the grateful king.

E Forth Rail Bridge
Completed in 1890, the bridge took seven years to construct and was a great achievement of

19th-century engineering. There is an exhibition on the bridge at the north side, in the Queensferry Lodge Hotel. Telephone (01383) 417759 for information.

Food and drink

There are pubs, restaurants and convenience stores in South Queensferry and Davidson's Mains, a pub at Cramond Brig and a convenience store in Dalmeny. Refreshments are also available at Hopetoun House and Dalmeny House.

☕ **Coffee Room, South Queensferry**
Popular with cyclists, serving tea, coffee, light meals and ice cream.

☕ **Village Tea Room, Davidson's Mains**
Tea, coffee, sandwiches and soup.

🍺 **Village Inn, Davidson's Mains**
Morning coffee available from 1000, meals served all day.

Route description

If parking in supermarket car park, either carry bike up steps at south end of the car park and TR into Morison Gardens, or, ride round – TR out of car park, TR into The Loan and TR again into Morison Gardens (no SP).

Cycle down Morison Gardens, heading towards the Forth Road Bridge. TL at foot of hill, into Hopetoun Road. TR at XR, SP Hopetoun House. Continue on road as it descends to and alongside seashore. Views of estuary and, in the distance, the Ochil Hills and Longannet Power Station.

1 SO where road forks, SP Welcome to Hopetoun. Cycle through ornamental gateway for steady climb through trees. Continue SO through small gates. Follow road to left and keep SO at ticket booth, keeping walled garden on left. Cross cattle grid. *4km (2.5 miles)*

2 Follow road as it turns right, through parkland to western gate. TL at TJ, no SP, for stiff climb. At cottages follow road to right and climb gently.

3 SO at staggered XR with A904, SP Winchburgh. Pass Duntarvie Tower (a ruin now being restored) on right and TL at TJ, SP Hopetoun Fishery. Continue SO at all junctions, until you arrive at XR with A904.

4 SO at XR across bottom of triangle, then TR into wide road (old South Queensferry road), no SP. *10.5km (6.5 miles)*

5 TR at XR under road bridge into Stewart Terrace, which becomes Loch Road. RHF at top of Loch Road, into Kirkliston Road. Continue to just before roundabout and TL into Scotstoun Avenue. Continue.

6 Road ends at factory entrance. Take track on right (tarmac) and follow round to right (14km/8.5 miles). TL at TJ of tracks, into old road lined with trees. Continue to end, go round gates and SO onto minor road into Dalmeny village. Keep SO, SP Edinburgh B924.

7 TR at XR, no SP (SO is entrance to Dalmeny House). Continue on pavement (officially shared-use) where B road joins A90. Exit onto slip road and SO at TJ, SP Check Point – the road becomes one-way. Continue onto cycle track when it starts on left at old weighbridge. As cycle track ends, go through car park of Cramond Brig pub, keeping off A90 for as long as possible. From car park, either ride along A90 or walk along pavement for 150m.

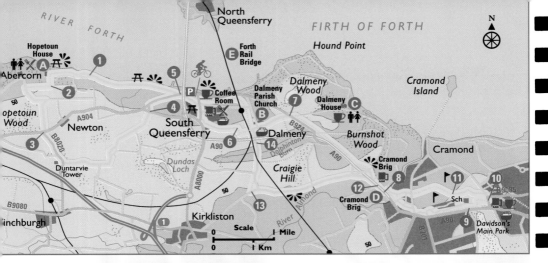

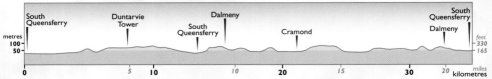

8 TL past barrier into Braehead Avenue. Then first TR (after post box), into Braehead Road, no SP. At end of road, TR into Whitehouse Road, no SP. Pass shops on left and TL into Barnton Grove. TL again into Barnton Park View, then TR into Barnton Park Wood. At end of road, cycle SO onto track between fences and continue into wood. Follow track as it runs parallel to A90, separated by high wall (20km/12.5 miles). SO across residential road, no SP.

9 SO at XR of paths, no SP. Pass Royal High School on left. LHF at junction of tracks, and into Davidson's Main park where TL onto tarmac. TR at TJ of tracks, keeping park on right and passing park building.

10 LHF to exit park and TR into East Barnton Avenue, no SP. Pass gateway and TL into Cramond Road South for 100m. TL into Barnton Avenue, SP Cramond Brig. Continue.

11 Road ends and SO onto track, past barrier. Follow track as it goes between two golf courses. Exit into Barnton Avenue West and

SO. SO at XR into Braepark Road, SP Cramond Brig.

12 Arrive Cramond Brig (25km/15.5 miles). Climb past pub on short section of old road for 200m, and look for cycle track. Cross road next to old weighbridge and take underpass under main road. Loop round to left onto A90, keeping inside protective lane as you go uphill. Then, LHF, SP Kirkliston. Views of airport and Pentland Hills. Continue. After cutting, go under railway.

13 TR onto track immediately before old railway bridge, SP Dalmeny. Beware – loose gravel. TR and continue along old rail track (29km/18 miles). At end of track continue SO onto minor road. Pass under railway and continue for 200m.

14 TL onto cycle track, SP Dalmeny Station. TR at caravans and continue under A90 to rail viaduct. For a good view of the Forth Rail Bridge, TR for short distance. Otherwise, continue on main track into South Queensferry. Track becomes tarmac and, after 400m, ends in supermarket carpark. **33.5km (21 miles)**

KELSO, MELLERSTAIN HOUSE AND HUME CASTLE

Route information

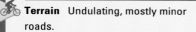

Distance   35km (21.5 miles)

Grade   Moderate

Terrain   Undulating, mostly minor roads.

Time to allow   3 hours.

Getting there by car   Kelso is 68km (42m) south east of Edinburgh, via the A68, A697 and A6089. There is car parking behind Kelso Abbey next to the Old Parish Church (large octagonal-shaped building). There is a path from the car park, past the Abbey, into Bridge Street where TR for square.

Getting there by train   There is no railway service to Kelso but some buses from Edinburgh will carry bicycles. For information, telephone Lowland Buses on 0131 663 1945.

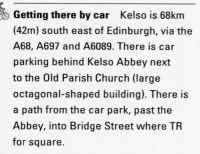

From Kelso along part of the Tweed Cycleway, the route climbs out of the Tweed valley to Smailholm, with its prominent tower, and continues to the stately home of Mellerstain and dramatic Hume Castle, perched high over the surrounding countryside. The return route passes through the attractive villages of Stichill and Ednam.

Places of interest along the route

A Kelso

Kelso sits at the junction of the Tweed and Teviot Rivers. The five-arched bridge over the Tweed was built in 1803 by John Rennie and was the model for London Bridge. **Kelso Abbey**, founded in 1128, suffered in the Border wars and today only magnificent ruins remain. Historic Scotland property. Access at all reasonable times. Admission free. Telephone 0131 668 8800. **Kelso Museum** describes Kelso's history as a market town and skinning and tanning centre. Also displays on archaeology and the Abbey. The adjacent Turret Gallery holds changing exhibitions. Gift shop. Open July and August, 1000–1200 and 1400–1600. Admission free. Telephone (01573) 225470. **Floors Castle**, home of the Roxburgh family, contains outstanding French 17th- and 18th-century furniture, art, tapestries and porcelain. Extensive parkland and walled gardens. Gift shop, tearoom and picnic area. Open Easter to October, daily 1000–1630. Charge. Telephone (01573) 223333.

B Smailholm Tower, near Kelso

A well-preserved 16th-century Border peel tower containing an exhibition of costume and tapestries relating to Sir Walter Scott's *Minstrelsy* of the Scottish Borders. Historic Scotland property. Open April to September, Monday–Saturday 0930–1830, Sunday 1400–1830. Charge. Telephone (01573) 460365.

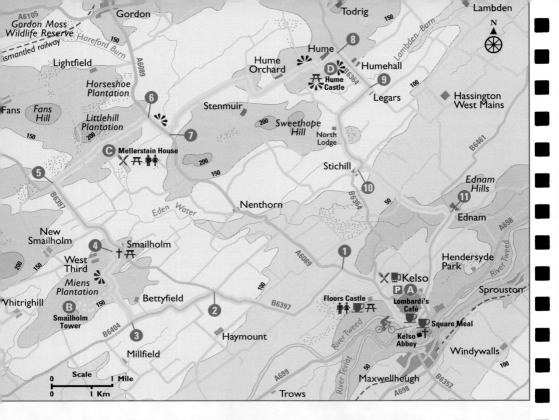

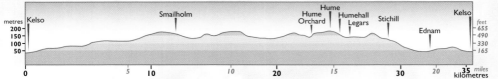

Ⓒ Mellerstain House, Gordon, near Kelso

A superb Georgian mansion designed by William and Robert Adam. Features exquisite plaster ceilings, beautiful interior decoration, fine period furniture and a marvellous art collection. Also terraced garden. Gift shop, restaurant and picnic area. Open Easter and May to September, Sunday–Friday 1230–1700. Charge. Telephone (01573) 410225.

Ⓓ Hume Castle, Hume, near Kelso

The original seat of the Home family. The castle was used as a beacon to warn of invasion, and was the only castle not destroyed by Robert Bruce's scorched earth policy in 1313. It was eventually destroyed by Cromwell and was later partly rebuilt. Used again as a beacon in the Napoleonic Wars, the warning fire was accidentally lit and caused national pandemonium. Stunning views of the Cheviots and the Tweed valley. Open all year, daily 0900–2100. Admission free. For further information, telephone Kelso Tourist Information Centre on (01573) 223464.

Route description

Start from the square in the centre of Kelso. Take Roxburgh Street (south west corner of square, one-way). TL at TJ onto A6089 SP Edinburgh and pass entrance to Floors Castle.

1 TL at TJ, SP Smailholm B6397 (2.5km/1.5 miles). Cycle past wall of Floors Castle Estate on left and continue for steady climb.

2 TL at XR, SP St Boswells B6404. Continue. *7km (4.5 miles)*

3 TR at TJ, SP Smailholm Tower. Climb and pass track to Smailholm Tower on left. View from summit of Eildon Hills.

4 Arrive Smailholm. TR at TJ for 50m, SP Mellerstain. TL onto main road, SP Earlston B6397 (picnic spot opposite attractive Smailholm Church). Continue on B6397. *12km (7.5 miles)*

5 TR at TJ, SP Mellerstain, for gentle climb past entrance to Mellerstain House. Continue. *16km (10 miles)*

6 TR at triangular TJ, SP Kelso A6089. View on left of Hume Castle. Descend to the Eden Water.

7 TL at TJ, SP Hume (18.5km/11.5 miles). Continue past Hume Castle and into Hume village. *23.5km (14.5 miles)*

8 TR at TJ, SP Kelso, for long descent.

9 TR at TJ, following main road. Pass North Lodge. Then short sharp climb and descent to Stichill.

10 Arrive Stichill. SO to visit village. Otherwise, TL at TJ, SP Ednam, for long descent to Ednam. *31.5km (19.5 miles)*

11 TR at TJ, SP Kelso, and return to Kelso to complete the route, following SP Town Centre. *35km (21.5 miles)*

Food and drink

This route is rural and there are no refreshment facilities other than those in Kelso (several cafés, tearooms and pubs) and at Floors Castle and Mellerstain House.

Lombardi's Café, Kelso
The usual range of café fare.

Square Meal, Kelso
Serving tea, coffee, soup, filled rolls and baked potatoes.

Smailholm Tower

Route 9
JEDBURGH AND THE JED VALLEY

Route information

Distance   37km (23 miles)

Grade   Strenuous

Terrain   The two big climbs early in the ride, one out of Jedburgh and the other, less severe, from Crailinghall, warrant the strenuous grade, but the rest of the route is quite moderate, though still hilly. Mostly minor roads, but short sections on the busy A698. Two off-road sections. Suitable for most bicycles with gears to cope with the hills.

Time to allow   4–5 hours.

Getting there by car   Jedburgh is 80km (49.5 miles) south of Edinburgh on the A68. Park at the south end of the town in the Old Toll car park, beside SP Last Shop in Scotland, where A68 crosses river.

Getting there by train   There are no rail services to Jedburgh, but some buses from Edinburgh carry bicycles. For more information, telephone Lowland Buses on 0131 663 1945.

A challenging ride through superb, but hilly countryside north east of Jedburgh. The route crosses a footbridge on the splendid Roxburgh railway viaduct, over the River Teviot. The return is over Roxburgh Moor, with fine views, and passes the Waterloo Monument on Peniel

Heugh (236m/741 feet above sea level). The monument was built in 1815 by the Marquis of Lothian and his tenants in memory of the Duke of Wellington. The pine trees are said to represent French troops, the hardwood trees the British army. The final section of the route returns to Jedburgh on a hilly, minor road through the Jed valley.

Places of interest along the route

A Jedburgh

A settlement was established at Jedburgh in 54 AD by the Bishop of Lindisfarne. Jedburgh's position as a frontier town on the English/Scottish border meant that it was in the midst of battles and cross-border raids. **Jedburgh Abbey**, High Street, was one of the four great Borders Abbeys founded by David I circa 1138. It was repeatedly attacked by English armies and was finally devastated in 1545. A way-marked route takes visitors around the remarkable Romanesque and Gothic ruins and a visitor centre portrays life in the monastery. Historic Scotland property. Gift shop, tearoom and picnic area. Open April to September, Monday–Saturday 0930–1800, Sunday 1400–1830; October to March, Monday–Saturday 0930–1830, Sunday 1400–1630. Charge. Telephone (01835) 863925. **Mary, Queen of Scots' House**, Queen Street, is a 15th-century castle, now a visitor centre telling the story of the Queen's turbulent life. Gift shop. Open Easter to October, Monday–Saturday 1000–1645, Sunday 1000–1630. Charge. Telephone (01835) 863331. The **Castle Jail and Museum**,

Castle Gate, is located in the old Reform Prison, dating from 1824 and designed to the principles of the prison reformer John Howard. Displays on the history of Jedburgh and a museum of social history. Gift shop and picnic area. Open all year, Monday–Saturday 1000–1630, Sunday 1300–1600. Charge. Telephone (01835) 863254.

B Teviot Water Gardens, near Jedburgh

Water gardens on four levels, set amidst scenic Borders countryside. The lowest garden runs down to the River Teviot. Also smokery in 18th-century coaching inn. Gift shop and tearoom. Open April to September, daily 1000–1700. Admission free. Telephone (01835) 850634.

C Monteviot House Garden, near Jedburgh

On the banks of the River Teviot, comprising river garden, rose terraces and water garden. Open April to October, Monday–Friday 1200–1700. Charge. Telephone (01835) 830380.

D Harestanes Countryside Visitor Centre, Ancrum, near Jedburgh

Indoor and outdoor activities with changing exhibitions, waymarked walks and wildlife garden. Gift shop, tearoom and picnic area. Open April to October, daily 1000–1700. Admission free; charge for activities. Telephone (01835) 830306.

Jedburgh

Route description

Leave Old Toll car park and cross A68 into Oxnam Road, SP Oxnam. Immediately start to climb. Views left over Jedburgh and, further up, south up Jed valley.

1 TL at TJ, SP Crailinghall, for more climbing. Views north and south. Reach summit for steep descent to Crailinghall, then climb to:

2 TL at XR, SP Heiton, for more climbing (excellent views) then long descent.
5.5km (3.5 miles)

3 TR at TJ, SP Kelso A698, for 300m. TR at TJ (with care), SP Eckford, and continue through village.

4 TL at XR onto B6401, no SP (11km/7 miles), and continue to Kalemouth.

5 To visit Teviot Water Gardens, TL at TJ for 20m. Otherwise, to continue route, TR at TJ into cycle lane, SP Heiton A698. Cross Kale Water and continue.

6 TL at SP Sunlaws House Hotel, through gates, past lodge, onto track through woods (13km/8 miles). At Hotel, exit from track onto tarmac, TR and follow main drive to northern exit and gates (golf course on left).

7 TL sharply at gates, SP No Exit, and descend to river and viaduct.

8 TL at railway viaduct, onto footbridge, and cross River Teviot. Continue SO on footpath and, at end, SO onto minor road for 300m, no SP (but SP Roxburgh to right). TL at TJ, SP St Boswells, and climb. *17km (10.5 miles)*

9 TL at TJ at summit, height restriction SP only. View of Waterloo Monument on left.
19km (12 miles)

10 TL at TJ, no SP. Then, TL at TJ (effectively SO). Keep left at Fairnington Lodge.
24km (15 miles)

11 TL at TJ, no SP.

12 TL at TJ – easy to miss, no SP, but post with red direction arrows into minor road (25km/15.5m). Descend. Pass entrance to Peniel Heugh and Waterloo Monument on left (steep track). Continue descent.

13 At foot of hill, to visit Monteviot House Garden and Harestanes Countryside Visitor Centre, TR at TJ, both places signed. Otherwise, to continue route, TL at TJ, no SP. Continue to Nisbet.

14 Arrive Nisbet. TR to follow main road, SP Crailing.

15 TR at TJ, SP Jedburgh A698 (31.5km/ 19.5 miles). Pass Mounthooly Farm (Caddy Mann Tearoom) on right.

16 TL at TJ, SP 4 Abbeys and St Cuthbert's Way. Continue.

17 TL at TJ onto A68. Immediately TL into residential road, SP 4 Abbeys (35km/21.5 miles). Bear right into Forthill Terrace, SP 4 Abbeys. Reach A68 and bear left into Waterside. SO at mini roundabout for 50m. TR to riverside and bear left over footbridge. TL along riverside walk (partly track). Go under subway and TL into car park to finish the route.
37km (23 miles)

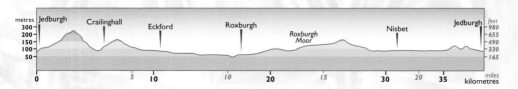

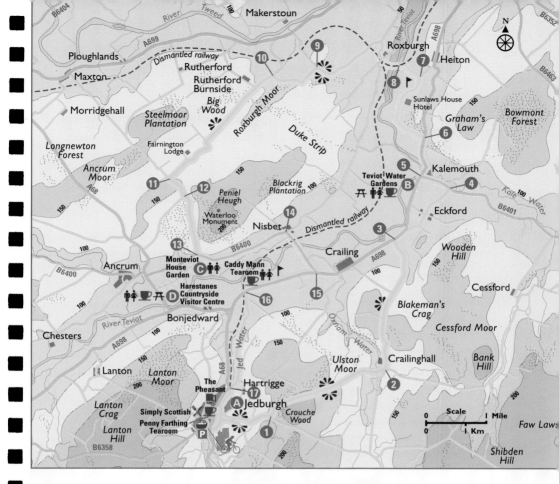

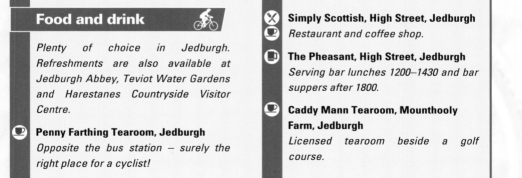

Food and drink 🚴

Plenty of choice in Jedburgh. Refreshments are also available at Jedburgh Abbey, Teviot Water Gardens and Harestanes Countryside Visitor Centre.

☕ **Penny Farthing Tearoom, Jedburgh**
Opposite the bus station – surely the right place for a cyclist!

❌☕ **Simply Scottish, High Street, Jedburgh**
Restaurant and coffee shop.

🍺 **The Pheasant, High Street, Jedburgh**
Serving bar lunches 1200–1430 and bar suppers after 1800.

☕ **Caddy Mann Tearoom, Mounthooly Farm, Jedburgh**
Licensed tearoom beside a golf course.

COLDSTREAM AND THE TWEED CYCLEWAY

Route information

Distance 38km (23.5 miles)

Grade Easy

Terrain Minor roads through the Tweed valley, with some steady climbs.

Time to allow 3–4 hours.

Getting there by car Coldstream is west of the A1 on the A698 and A697. There is car parking off the High Street, in Market Square.

Getting there by train The nearest railway station is at Berwick-upon-Tweed, 7km (4.5 miles) from the northernmost point of ride. Leave Berwick on the A698 and after 4.5km (3 miles) TR onto minor road, SP Horncliffe. Cycle through Horncliffe and start the route at direction 6.

This route travels through the quiet and unspoilt countryside of the Tweed valley, generally on the Tweed Cycleway, from the border town of Coldstream, to Ladykirk, Paxton and then back through the ancient village of Norham.

Route description

From the car park, head north east along the High Street towards the Tweed Bridge. Bear left onto A6112, SP Duns. Continue on this road into the village of Lennel.

1 TL at TJ, SP Oxenrig. Then, TR at TJ, no SP but view of Oxenrig Farm ahead. Continue to XR where SO, SP Tweed Cycleway. Stay on this road, passing distinctive stone lions at entrance to Ladykirk Estate. *7km (4.5 miles)*

2 TR at TJ, SP Ladykirk. Continue through Upsettlington and follow road as it turns sharp left and then bears right.

3 SO at XR, SP Tweed Cycleway (10km/ 6 miles). Pass Ladykirk Church on left. Continue on this road through the hamlet of Horndean.

4 TR at TJ, SP Berwick B6461, and continue.

5 To visit Paxton House, bear left at TJ for 1.5km (1 mile). Otherwise, to continue route, bear right at TJ, SP Horncliffe. Continue to cross Union Suspension Bridge (17.5km/ 11 miles). Pass Chainbridge Honey Farm on left.

6 To return to Berwick-upon-Tweed, TL at TJ and retrace route along Tweed Cycleway and A698. Otherwise, to continue route TR at TJ, SP Horncliffe. Continue through Horncliffe. *19km (12 miles)*

7 TR at TJ, SP Norham, and continue through Norham.

8 TR at TJ onto B6470, SP Ladykirk. Continue on this road, descend across the River Tweed, and SO at XR, staying on B6470.

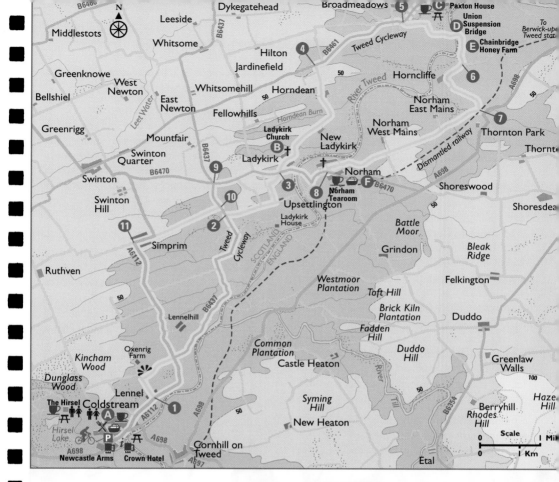

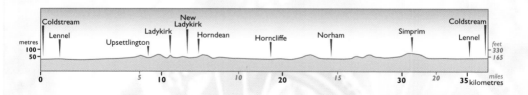

9 TL at XR, SP Coldstream B6437.

10 TR at TJ, no SP (on downhill, by isolated tree – 30.5km/19 miles) and continue SO. SO at TJ, SP Coldstream A6112.

11 TL at TJ, following A6112 back to Coldstream and the end of the route.

38km (23.5 miles)

Places of interest along the route

A Coldstream

The bridge in Coldstream marks the Scottish–English border. The town is well known as the birthplace of the Coldstream Guards, formed in 1660. **Coldstream Museum**, Market Square, contains an exhibition on the regiment, as well as local history. Gift shop and picnic area. Open April to September, Monday–Saturday 1000–1600, Sunday 1400–1600; October, Monday–Wednesday and Saturday 1000–1200 and 1400–1600. Charge. Telephone (01890) 882630. **The Hirsel**, on the outskirts of Coldstream, is the home of the Douglas-Home family. The house is not open to the public but the grounds contain a local history museum, craft centre and country park. Tearoom and picnic area. Grounds open all year, daily, sunrise–dusk; museum, craft centre and tearoom open all year, Monday–Friday 1000–1700, weekends 1200–1700. Charge for admission to museum. Telephone (01890) 882834.

B Ladykirk Church, Ladykirk

Unusually built completely from stone – even the roof and, until earlier this century, the pews. The church was designed to be fire and flood proof, being so close to the border and the Tweed, and the risk of raids and flooding. Open at all reasonable times. Admission by donation. For further information, telephone the Tourist Information Centre in Coldstream on (01890) 882607.

C Paxton House, Paxton

A fine 18th-century country house containing the largest collection of Chippendale furniture in Scotland, and as an outstation of the National Galleries of Scotland, a large art gallery. Also extensive gardens and parkland. Gift shop, tearoom and picnic area. Open Easter to October, daily 1000–1730. Charge. Telephone (01289) 386291.

D Union Suspension Bridge, near Paxton

This suspension bridge, the first of its type in the country, was built by Samuel Brown in 1820. Access at all reasonable times. Free.

E Chainbridge Honey Farm, Horncliffe

Honey farm established in 1966 and open to the public. Observation hides, visitor centre, and gift shop. Open April to October, Monday–Friday 1000–1700, Saturday 1100–1730, Sunday 1400–1730; November to December, Saturday 1100–1730, Sunday 1400–1700. Admission free. Telephone (01289) 386362.

F Norham

The first Norham Castle was built of wood by Bishop Flambard in 1121, probably on the site of a previously fortified area. The present castle was built between 1158 and 1174, and from then until 1603 it was besieged 14 times and captured seven times, with much re-building. After 1603 it fell into disrepair and was cannibalised for the older houses in the village. Part of the Parish Church was constructed in the 12th century, also by Bishop Flambard. The remains of an older Saxon church lie in the trees 50m to the east.

Food and drink

Plenty of choice at Coldstream. Refreshments are also available at The Hirsel, Paxton House and in Norham, where there are convenience stores.

Crown Hotel, Market Square, Coldstream
Bar lunches available.

Newcastle Arms, High Street, Coldstream
A wide range of bar meals available, with tea and coffee served all day.

Norham Tearoom, Norham
Popular with cyclists. Closed Monday.

THE TWEED VALLEY – GALASHIELS TO WALKERBURN

Route information

 Distance 39km (24 miles)

Grade Moderate

Terrain Quite hilly on the outward section; the return is over undulating minor roads and a short off-road section suitable for most bicycles.

Time to allow 4 hours.

Getting there by car Galashiels is 53km (33 miles) south of Edinburgh on the A7. There is a car park at the south east end of the one-way system – TL, SP Currie Road, then TR by church into car park by old station.

Getting there by train There are no rail services to Galashiels, but some buses from Edinburgh carry bicycles. For more information, telephone Lowland Buses on 0131 663 1945.

From Galashiels this route heads west along the Tweed valley to Walkerburn and then returns through Elibank Forest and past Ashiestiel, home of Sir Walter Scott before he built Abbotsford. Ashiestiel Bridge, the first crossing of the river after Walkerburn, was built in 1847, when it was the largest single-span, rubble arch bridge in the world at 40m (132 feet). Much of the route follows the Tweed Cycleway.

Places of interest along the route

Ⓐ Galashiels

The prosperity of Galashiels was built on the textile industry – the motto of the Galashiels Manufacturer's Corporation was 'we dye to live and live to die'. The **Loch Carron Cashmere and Wool Centre**, Waverley Mill, Huddersfield Street, offers visitors tours explaining the weaving process and contains a museum illustrating the history of Galashiels and its trade. Gift shop. Open June to September, Monday–Saturday 0900–1700, Sunday 1200–1700. Charge for tour, otherwise admission free. Telephone (01896) 751100. **Old Gala House**, Scotts Crescent, was the former home of the Lairds of Gala and now contains displays on the house itself, its inhabitants and the early history of Galashiels, and an art gallery. Gardens open to visitors. Tearoom. Open April to October, Tuesday–Saturday 1000–1600. Admission free. Telephone (01896) 752611.

Food and drink

There are several nice cafés in Galashiels, in Bank Street and Green Street, pubs serving bar meals, restaurants and convenience stores. The Mill Shop in Walkerburn has a coffee shop, and refreshments are available at Old Gala House.

Clovenfords Hotel, Clovenfords
Bar meals served.

George Hotel, Walkerburn
Food available.

Route description

TR out of old Galashiels Station car park and join main one-way system through the town, SO following SP A72 Peebles/Walkerburn. Continue for 5km (3 miles) along A72 to Clovenfords.

1 Arrive Clovenfords. TR at roundabout, SP Bowland B710 for quite a steep climb.

6km (3.5 miles)

2 TL at TJ near top of hill into minor road, SP Ferniehirst. Cycle over summit for gentle descent through fine pastoral landscape.

3 TL at TJ, SP Thornylee. Climb again, then long descent (with fine views of Tweed valley) to A72 at Thornylee.

4 TR at TJ, SP Peebles A72 (11km/7 miles). The A72 is not usually busy, but take care as it is narrow in places. Continue to Walkerburn.

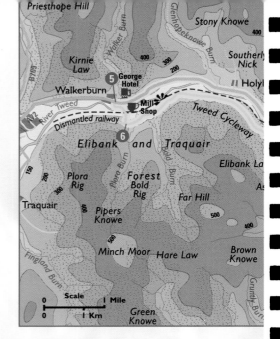

Galashiels

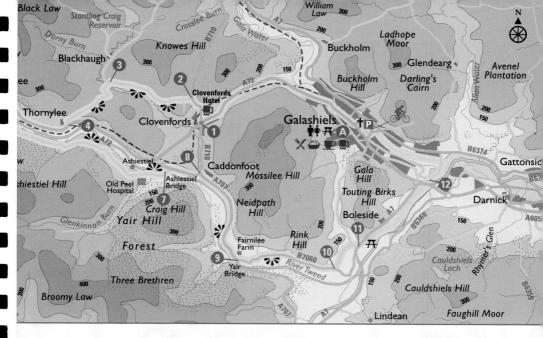

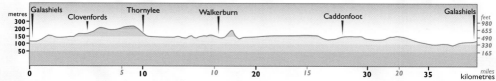

5 Easy to miss – TL at TJ, no SP, into Caberston Road (where main road bends right and crosses burn). Cross River Tweed.

6 TL at TJ, SP Elibank (17km/10.5 miles). Route from here follows the Tweed Cycleway, alongside the River Tweed. Road climbs into forest, descends then climbs again. Pass Ashiestiel, now a farm (25km/15.5 miles). Descend, with sharp left bend part of the way down, then pass old Peel Hospital – beware of vehicles emerging from hidden driveways.

7 Cross river at Ashiestiel Bridge. TR at TJ. Almost immediately TR again onto A707, SP Tweed Cycleway.

8 Follow main road (A707) round to right, SP Selkirk. Cycle into Caddonfoot where follow main road to right. Continue on A707 to Fairnilee and Yair Bridge.

9 TL at TJ before Yair Bridge, SP Galashiels B7060 (29.5km/18.5 miles). Climb out of valley (good views to right). As road descends, look out for:

10 TL at TJ onto minor road, SP Tweed Cycleway. Continue and TR at TJ, SP Tweed Cycleway.

11 TL at TJ (with care) onto A7 for 30m. TR onto old road, starting as track and going downhill on right, SP Tweed Cycleway. Pass picnic areas beside river and continue on Tweed Cycleway.

12 Arrive mini roundabout at high-level road bridge. SO into Winston Road for 700m. TL onto old railway track, no SP but SP to right Tweed Cycleway (37km/23 miles). Follow track back to old Galashiels Station car park to complete the route. **39km (24 miles)**

COLDINGHAM, EYEMOUTH AND THE WHITEADDER VALLEY

Route information

Distance 39.5km (24.5 miles)

Grade Moderate

Terrain Undulating coastal roads and inland lanes, but no major climbs.

Time to allow 3–4 hours.

Getting there by car Coldingham is 72km (44.5 miles) east of Edinburgh on the north east coast, via the A1 and A1107. There is a car park beside the Public Hall in the centre of Coldingham.

Getting there by train The nearest railway station is Berwick-upon-Tweed, 8km (5 miles) from Foulden. TL out of the station and follow A6105 to Foulden, where SO through village at direction 6.

A route along almost traffic-free roads, through pleasant rolling countryside. From Coldingham the route heads along the coast to the village of Eyemouth. From here you turn inland, over the hills and along the Whiteadder Valley, passing Hutton Castle, once the home of Sir William Burrell who amassed the Burrell Collection, now in Glasgow. The route returns to Coldingham through Chirnside and Reston.

Places of interest along the route

A Eyemouth

Five miles north of the border lies Eyemouth, a fishing village since the 13th century. Today it is also a popular tourist destination with its natural harbour and sandy beaches. The **Eyemouth Museum** commemorates a terrible fishing disaster of 1881 when 189 men were lost at sea, and illustrates the local farming, mining and fishing industries. Gift shop. Open April to June and September, Monday–Saturday 1000–1700, Sunday 1400–1600; July and August, Monday–Saturday 1000–1800, Sunday 1100–1600; October, Monday–Saturday 1000–1230 and 1330–1630. Charge. Telephone (01890) 750678.

B Ayton Castle, near Eyemouth

Victorian castle dating from 1846. It has been restored and is lived in as a family home. Conducted tours and woodland walks. Gift shop. Open May to September, Sunday 1300–1700, and at other times by appointment. Charge. Telephone (01890) 781212.

C Foulden Tithe Barn, near Chirnside

An ancient, two-storey stone barn with outside stair and stepped gables, where tithes (ten per cent of local produce) were stored. Historic Scotland property. View exterior only. Access at all reasonable times. For further information, telephone Historic Scotland on 0131 668 8800.

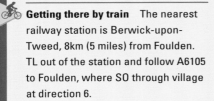

Rolling fields, the Borders

Food and drink

There are convenience stores in Coldingham and Reston, and plenty of choice for refreshment in Eyemouth and Chirnside.

Anchor Inn, High Street, Coldingham
Bar lunches and afternoon teas.

Contented Sole, Harbour Road, Eyemouth
Pub serving tea and coffee and bar lunches.

Old Bakehouse, Eyemouth
Serves coffee, lunch and afternoon tea.

The Wheatsheaf, Reston
Bar meals available.

Route description

From the centre of Coldingham village, TL onto A1107. Continue on this road following SP Eyemouth. As road climbs, views behind of St Abbs and rocky headlands.

1 TL at foot of hill, SP Town Centre, and cycle into Eyemouth. Follow one-way system along High Street and pass Museum on left. TL for harbour. Otherwise, continue to end of town where TR, then keep left, SP Burnmouth A1107.
6.5km (4 miles)

2 SO at XR, SP Ayton B6355. Cross stream for long climb.

3 At summit, cycle across bridge over A1. Continue into Ayton, passing Ayton Castle on left.

4 TL at TJ, SP Chirnside. Cross Eye Water. TR at TJ, SP Chirnside, for steady climb to railway bridge. *12km (7.5 miles)*

5 TL at TJ by railway bridge, SP Foulden, for more climbing. View behind of Ayton and Coldingham Moor. Summit of hill at grove of beech trees with view ahead of Cheviot Hills (16km/10 miles). Descend to Foulden.

6 If returning to Berwick-upon-Tweed station, TL and continue on A6105 to Berwick-upon-Tweed.

Otherwise, to continue route TR at TJ onto A6105, no SP. Pass Foulden Tithe Barn on left and continue through Foulden (good picnic spot). *18.5km (11.5 miles)*

7 TL at XR, SP Hutton. Continue to descend steeply to Whiteadder Water then climb out of gorge.

8 TR at TJ, SP Hutton.

9 Arrive Hutton. TR at TJ, no SP but where main road goes left (23.5km/14.5 miles). Pass church on right. Continue and pass entrance to Hutton Castle.

10 TR at TJ, no SP (reverse SP Hutton). Descend to Whiteadder valley, follow Whiteadder Water and cross by footbridge. Continue to junction with A6105.

11 TR at TJ onto main road for 20m, no SP. TL, SP Reston B6355 (28.5km/17.5 miles). TL at TJ at top of hill to visit shops in Chirnside. Otherwise, TR then TL at TJ, SP Reston B6437, and continue for more climbing.

12 TR at TJ, SP Reston, and continue towards village. *32km (20 miles)*

13 TL at TJ to visit Reston. Otherwise, TR at TJ, no SP. SO across A1 (with care) at staggered XR (35.5km/22 miles). After climb descend and climb again, back into Coldingham to complete the route. *39.5km (24.5 miles)*

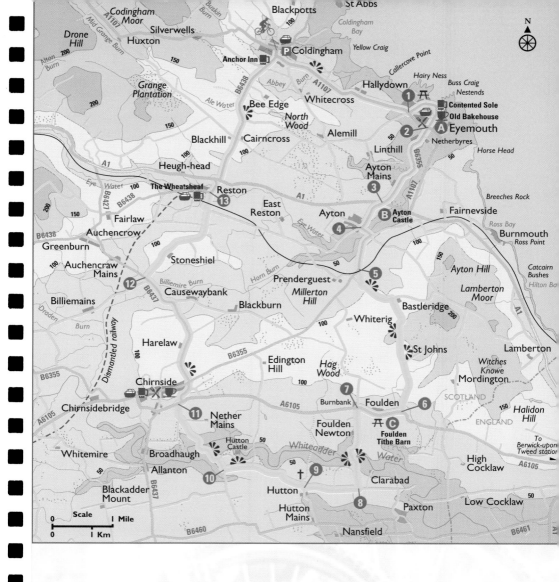

Codingham Moor
A1107
Buskin Burn
Blackpotts
St Abbs
100
Mid Grange Burn
Silverwells
Coldingham Bay
Drone Hill
Huxton
200
P Coldingham
Yellow Craig
Callercove Point
150
Anchor Inn
Abbey Burn
A1107
Hallydown
Hairy Ness
Buss Craig
Nestends
Hilton Burn
200
Eye Water
Grange Plantation
Ale Water
Whitecross
1
Contented Sole
Old Bakehouse
200
Bee Edge
North Wood
150
A1107
150
Alemill
2
A Eyemouth
150
Blackhill
Cairncross
Netherbyres
Horse Head
100
100
Heugh-head
Linthill
50
B6355
100
A1
A1
Ayton Mains
50
Breeches Rock
Eye Water
100
The Wheatsheaf
Reston
3
Fairnevside
Ross Bay
B6438
B6427
13
East Reston
Ayton
B Ayton Castle
Burnmouth
Ross Point
200
Fairlaw
150
Eye Water
4
100
Catcairn Bushes
Hilton Ba
B6438
Auchencrow
100
Ayton Hill
Greenburn
Stoneshiel
Horn Burn
50
150
100
Auchencraw Mains
5
Lamberton Moor
Billiemire Burn
12
Prenderguest
Millerton Hill
Bastleridge
200
B6437
Billiemains
Causewaybank
Blackburn
100
Whiterig
Lamberton
Droden Burn
Harelaw
100
B6355
Edington Hill
Hag Wood
St Johns
Witches Knowe
Mordington
100
B6355
Chirnside
100
A6105
Burnbank
7
Foulden
6
SCOTLAND
Halidon Hill
150
Chirnsidebridge
A6105
11
Nether Mains
Hutton Castle
50
Foulden Newton
C
Foulden Tithe Barn
ENGLAND
To Berwick-upon-Tweed station
A6105
Whitemire
Broadhaugh
Allanton
50
Whiteadder
Water
High Cocklaw
50
Blackadder Mount
10
9
Hutton
Clarabad
B6437
Hutton Mains
8
Paxton
Low Cocklaw
50
Scale
0   1 Mile
0   1 Km
B6460
Nansfield
B6461
A1

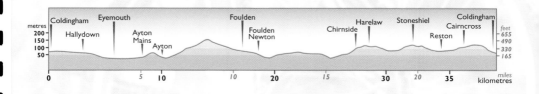

metres   Coldingham   Eyemouth   Foulden   Harelaw   Stoneshiel   Coldingham   feet
200 —   Hallydown   Ayton   Foulden   Chirnside   Reston   Cairncross   — 655
150 —   Mains   Ayton   Newton   — 490
100 —   — 330
50 —   — 165

0   5   10   10   20   15   30   20   35
miles
kilometres

WEST LOTHIAN CIRCUIT

Route information

 Distance   45km (28 miles)

Grade   Strenuous

Terrain   Minor roads and two lengthy off-road sections along a canal towpath and a cycle track. The first section of the route is hilly and quite strenuous, but from Beecraigs Country Park there is a long descent to Linlithgow and after that the route is only moderately hilly.

Time to allow   4–5 hours.

Getting there by car   Bathgate is 28km (17.5 miles) west of Edinburgh, off the M8 (junction 3a from the east, junction 4 from the west). There is a car park at Bathgate Station, in King Street near the town centre.

Getting there by train   There is a railway station at Bathgate, served by trains from Edinburgh. Bicycles are carried free. Telephone (0345) 484950 for information.

This route takes you through the varied country-side of West Lothian. From Bathgate north towards Linlithgow, and then south west to Avonbridge and Blackridge, before returning to Bathgate via a traffic-free cycle track, part of the National Cycle Network. En route, there are panoramic views of the Trossachs and Ben Lomond, two attractive country parks and a section alongside the Union Canal, passing by open moorland and woodland.

Places of interest along the route

Ⓐ Bathgate

Bathgate was a Medieval administrative centre and a staging post on the main Edinburgh to Glasgow road. The town expanded during the 18th and 19th centuries, first as a centre for handloom weaving and then through coal and shale mining, after James 'Paraffin' Young constructed his first paraffin refinery in 1850. The **Bennie Museum** contains almost 5000 artefacts illustrating the history of Bathgate, together with fossils and Roman glass and coins. Gift shop. Open April to September, Monday–Saturday 1000–1600; October to March, Monday–Saturday 1100–1530. Admission free. Telephone (01506) 634944.

Ⓑ Cairnpapple Hill, near Bathgate

One of the most important pre-historic monuments in Scotland, used as a burial and ceremonial site from around 3000 to 1400BC. There are excellent views from the site. Historic Scotland property. Access at all reasonable times. Free. Telephone (01506) 634622 for further information.

Ⓒ Beecraigs Country Park, near Linlithgow

Situated high in the Bathgate Hills, Beecraigs offers a wide range of recreational pursuits such as archery, fly fishing, bicycle trails and a deer farm. Visitor centre, gift shop, restaurant and picnic sites. Visitor centre open all year, Monday–Friday 0845–1200 and 1300–1600; park open at all reasonable times. Charge for some activities. Telephone (01506) 844516.

Ⓓ Linlithgow

The town was an ancient Royal Burgh and **Linlithgow Palace** is the magnificent ruin of the royal palace, set in its own park beside Linlithgow Loch. The palace was a favoured residence of the Stewart Monarchs and Mary, Queen of Scots was born here. Historic Scotland property. Gift shop and picnic area. Open April to September, Monday–Saturday 0930–1830, Sunday 1400–1830; October to March, Monday–Saturday 0930–1830, Sunday 1400–1630. Charge. Telephone (01506) 842896. **The Linlithgow Story**, High Street, housed in a late 18th-century merchant house, describes local history. Gift shop, picnic area and garden. Open April to October, Monday–Saturday (closed Tuesday) 1000–1700, Sunday 1300–1600. Charge. Telephone (01506) 670677. **Linlithgow Union Canal Society Museum**, in the canal basin, is situated in the former canal stables. Also canal cruises to the Avon Aqueduct. Gift shop, tearoom and picnic area. Open Easter to September, Saturday and Sunday 1400–1700. Admission to museum free, charge for boat trips. Telephone (01506) 671215.

Ⓔ Avon Aqueduct, Union Canal

The Union Canal opened in 1822 to connect Edinburgh with the Forth and Clyde Canal, enabling journeys between Glasgow and Edinburgh. One of three aqueducts on the Union Canal, the Avon is the largest aqueduct in Scotland, at 26m (86 feet) high and 247m (810 feet) long.

Ⓕ Muiravonside Country Park, near Linlithgow

Woodland, parkland and gardens covering 68ha (170 acres) of the Muiravonside Estate, formerly the home of the Stirling family. Visitor centre with local history exhibition. Also children's farm and dovecot. Tearoom open at weekends only. Open April to September, Monday–Friday 0900–1700, Sunday 1000–1800; October to March, weekends only 1000–1600. Admission free. Telephone (01506) 845311.

Avon Aqueduct

Food and drink

Lots of cafés, pubs, restaurants and convenience stores in Bathgate and Linlithgow. There are convenience stores in Avonbridge and Blackridge. Refreshments are also available at Beecraigs (off route) and Muiravonside Country Parks and in the Linlithgow Union Canal Society Museum.

Pete's Place, Bathgate
Café at the station entrance.

Coffee Club, George Street
Tea, coffee and snacks available.

Commercial Inn, Bathgate
Reasonably priced bar meals.

Route description

TL out of Bathgate Station for 30m, cross main road and go half right by clock into George Street (pedestrianised). Continue uphill through town centre. SO at XR into Livery Street.

1 TR at XR into Waverley Street. TL at roundabout, SP Bathgate Sports Centre. Continue for 200m. View ahead of Bathgate Hills – the route goes close to the mast on top!

2 TR at TJ onto minor road, SP Cathlaw, and select low gear for long climb along avenue of beech trees. At summit magnificent views: clockwise from north, Campsie Fells, Ben Lomond, Trossachs, Ben Ledi, Ben Vorlich, Ben Lawers (far background), Ochil Hills (3.5km/ 2 miles). Continue on road for long, steep descent.

3 TR (effectively SO) at TJ. Then TR at TJ, SP Cairnpapple. Track on right leads to summit of Cairnpapple Hill.

4 TL at TJ, SP Beecraigs Country Park. Short climb then short, steep descent (1:7) – beware sharp left bend, with potholes, at foot. Another short steep climb, with views east to Pentland Hills and Arthur's Seat, before entering woods to descend steadily. Pass entrances to Beecraigs Country Park (TR for adventure playground, information board and picnic area; TL for barbeque and another picnic area). *7km (4.5 miles)*

5 TR at TJ for 100m, no SP. TL (effectively SO) at TJ, SP Linlithgow. Continue towards Linlithgow for 1.5km (1 mile).

6 To visit Linlithgow, SO to bottom of hill and TR into High Street. After visit, retrace route and cross canal bridge. Otherwise, to continue route, halfway down hill (just after Priory Road), cross modern canal bridge and immediately TL onto canal towpath. Continue along towpath to Avon Aqueduct.

7 Cross Avon Aqueduct (cobbled surface). Continue on towpath as it enters wooded cutting and goes under bridge. TR after 20m, leaving towpath onto minor road. TR (double back) and go over bridge for 200m.

8 TL, SP Muiravonside Country Park, then SO to visitor centre. From visitor centre, retrace past car park and bear left up track through woodland, SP Alternate Exit. *16km (10 miles)*

9 Track ends at busy main road (A801). Cross with care and continue SO up minor road (almost opposite), SP Candie. Extensive views from Candiehead Farm.

10 TR at TJ at foot of hill for 300m, no SP. TL at TJ, no SP (after long, low modern house). Continue on steep descent (with sharp bends) into and then through valley.

11 TL at TJ onto B8028, no SP. Cross stream into Avonbridge. SO at TJ, SP Armadale. Climb short hill, cross narrow bridge over stream, pass houses on left and TR at TJ onto minor road, no SP (large, modern barn on left just after junction).

12 TR at TJ, SP Blackridge.
25km (15.5 miles)

13 Bear left at TJ, no SP, and climb gently, first through woodland and then over moorland, to a summit with extensive views (30km/ 18.5 miles). Descend into Blackridge.

14 SO (with care) across A89 XR, SP Harthill. At railway bridge, either scramble up bank (far side of bridge on right) onto tarmac track, or TR into Station Road for 150m, TR through barrier and TR (double back) when you reach tarmac track – this is part of the National Cycle Network. Follow track as it leaves bed of railway track and loops through old mine tailings. Continue on track, passing sculptures placed along the way.
35km (21.5 miles)

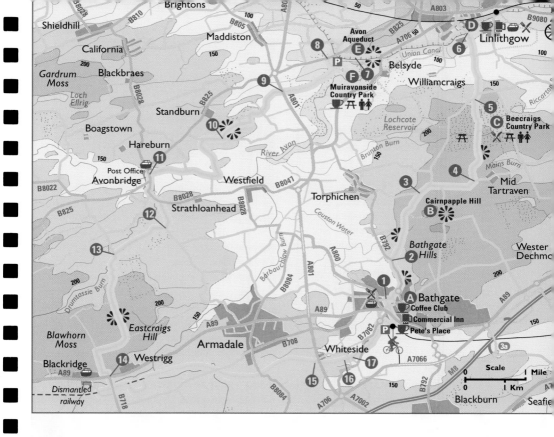

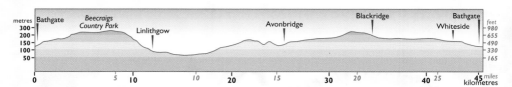

15 Take care here, just before Armadale Station, where a keyhole sculpture straddles the path, forming a potentially dangerous blind corner. Continue on track as it descends, crossing a rough farm track.

16 Cycle track leaves rail bed again and descends onto boggy ground, which can be deep after wet weather – you can use the railway track bed as an alternative here.

17 Tarmac track ends at Whiteside where TR into residential road. TL and follow road (parallel with railway) for 300m before continuing on track. RHF and track descends to pavement. Keep on this, past roundabout, cross road and SO for 200m. TR into Bathgate Retail Park and cross the car park for Bathgate Station and the end of the route.

45km (28 miles)

KELSO, YETHOLM AND THE TWEED VALLEY

Route information

Distance   46km (28.5 miles)

Grade   Moderate

Terrain   Undulating and at times hilly, quiet roads with one short section of off-road track, suitable for most bicycles.

Time to allow   3–4 hours.

Getting there by car   Kelso is 68km (42 miles) south east of Edinburgh, via the A68, A697 and A6089. There is a car park behind Kelso Abbey, next to the old parish church. A path from the car park passes the abbey into Bridge Street, where TR for the town centre or TL to start the route.

Getting there by train   There is no rail service to Kelso. However, some buses from Edinburgh will carry bicycles. For more information, telephone Lowland Buses on 0131 663 1945.

This route takes you briefly across the border into England. From Kelso the route climbs out of the Tweed valley to Wark Common and descends to East Learmouth. On to Branxton, Thornington and Kilham and then the route winds along the foot of the Cheviots to Yetholm. From here there is a climb back into the Tweed valley, finishing with a descent back into Kelso. The attractive scenery (with good picnic spots) and almost traffic-free roads make for excellent cycling.

Places of interest along the route

A Kelso

Kelso sits at the once strategically important point where the River Tweed meets the River Teviot. Its short distance from the border meant that, like many towns and villages close by, it suffered greatly during the Border conflicts. **Kelso Abbey**, Bridge Street, originally brought the town economic wealth. One of the four great Abbeys founded by David I, this was possibly the largest of them all. However, by 1587 there were only ruins left. Historic Scotland property. Open at all reasonable times. Admission free. Telephone 0131 668 8800 for further information. **Kelso Museum**, Abbey Court, illustrates the town's history, in particular the Abbey, archaeology, industry and agriculture. Also gallery with changing exhibitions. Gift shop. Open July and August, Monday–Saturday 1000–1200 and 1400–1600. Admission free. Telephone (01573) 225470.

B Flodden Field

Site of the Battle of Flodden (1513), when the Scottish army, despite massive support from both Highlanders and Lowlanders, were beaten by the English, with much loss of life on both sides. An information board gives a comprehensive account of the battle. Access at all reasonable times. Admission free.

C Cement Menagerie, Branxton

The creation of one man in his garden – cement deer, lions, bulls, Winston Churchill complete with cigar and Victory sign, a knight on horseback, and amusing notices. A gem of a place. Open when signposted. Admission by donation. For further information, telephone the Tourist Information Centre in Coldstream on (01890) 882607.

Food and drink

Kelso has several cafés, tearooms and pubs and a convenience store. There are convenience stores in Cornhill on Tweed and Town Yetholm.

Lombardi's Café, Kelso
The usual range of café fare.

Square Meal, Kelso
Serving tea, coffee, soup, filled rolls and baked potatoes.

Collingwood Arms, Cornhill on Tweed
Bar lunches and beer garden.

Border Hotel, Kirk Yetholm
Bar meals available at all times. Restaurant open on Saturday.

Plough Hotel, Town Yetholm
Good bar meals available at lunchtimes and in the evenings.

Near Kelso

Route description

Head along Bridge Street (south east corner of the town square). Pass Kelso Abbey on left, cross bridge, then bear left onto A698. As A698 goes right, TL into Sprouston Road. TL at end of road, no SP, and continue to Sprouston.

1   Arrive Sprouston. TR at end of village green (by cairn with lion rampant). Then TL into minor road (4.5km/3 miles). Continue for steady climb, passing hamlets of Kerchesters and Hadden.

2   SO onto track as road goes sharp left (at Nottylees), no SP. Descend gently with views of Tweed valley. Exit track onto minor road, keeping SO.   *10km (6 miles)*

3   TL at XR, SP East Learmouth, for sharp climb.

4   TL at TJ, SP East Learmouth.

5   Arrive East Learmouth. TL at TJ, SP Cornhill. To visit Cornhill continue SO into town. Otherwise, TR at TJ, SP Branxton and continue.   *15km (9.5 miles)*

6   TL at TJ, SP Branxton. Pass Flodden Field on right (good views and information board). Then pass Branxton church on left. RHF at TJ, broken SP for Crookham and Wooler.

7   TR at TJ, no SP but fountain and cement menagerie on left (19km/12 miles). Climb and continue on this road.

8   TR at TJ, SP Mindrum. Then SO at TJ, SP Yetholm. Descend steeply.

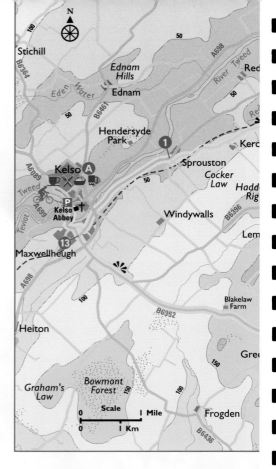

9   TR at TJ at foot of hill, SP Mindrum Mill B6352.   *24.5km (15 miles)*

10   Easy to miss – TL at TJ, no SP (triangular junction with SP Weak Bridge). Then TR at TJ, SP Yetholm. Stay on this road as it follows the Bowmont valley along the edge of the Cheviots and the Scottish–English border. Continue to Kirk Yetholm.

11   Arrive Kirk Yetholm and cycle through village to Town Yetholm.

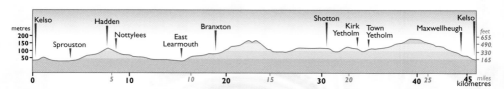

12 TR at TJ, no SP (or TL for pub and store). Then, TL at TJ, SP Kelso B6352 (34.5km/ 21.5 miles). Continue SO on B6352 with long climb to summit near Blakelaw Farm (40km/ 25 miles), then descent to Kelso.

13 Arrive Kelso and SO at A698. Descend to river and follow road across bridge to the Abbey and, behind it, the car park and the end of the route. *46km (28.5 miles)*

MUSSELBURGH TO HADDINGTON

From Musselburgh to Haddington on minor roads and traffic-free tracks. The grounds, garden and architecture of Lennoxlove House, passed en route, are among the finest in Scotland. Haddington, on the River Tyne, is a historic town, bypassed by main roads and full of Georgian charm. The return route is again almost entirely on minor roads, and the last section explores the coast and Port Seton harbour. Some of the traffic-free cycle tracks on this route were rebuilt by SPOKES, the volunteer Lothian Cycle Campaign.

Route information

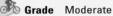

Distance 53km (33 miles)

Grade Moderate

Terrain A couple of climbs (one long and fairly steep early on in the route). Otherwise, fairly level on mostly minor roads. Two sections of traffic-free cycle track, suitable for most bicycles.

Time to allow 5–6 hours.

Getting there by car Musselburgh is 10km (6 miles) east of Edinburgh on the A199 and only 2km (1 mile) from the eastern end of the city bypass (A720). On Sundays it is possible to park beside the Town Hall. On other days, use the signed car park in Kerr's Wynd, just north of the Town Hall. Kerr's Wynd and the Town Hall are connected by a pedestrian path.

Getting there by train Musselburgh Railway Station, 2km (1 mile) from the centre of Musselburgh, is served by services from Edinburgh. From the station, TL at the top of Station Approach for 600m, TL at TJ then TR at next two sets of traffic lights into High Street, where continue to Town Hall. Telephone (0345) 484950 for timetable information.

Places of interest along the route

Ⓐ Inveresk Lodge Garden, Inveresk
Attractive terraced garden, owned by the National Trust for Scotland. The garden features a wide range of roses and shrubs and beautiful colour in autumn. There are fine views across the Esk Valley. Open April to September, Monday–Friday 1000–1630, weekends 1400–1700; October to March, Monday to Friday only. Charge. Telephone (01721) 722502.

Ⓑ Haddington
Once a royal burgh, Haddington was destroyed three times by the English during the 13th century border wars and again during the 14th century. The town also survived a 16-month long siege whilst it was occupied by the English in 1548–9. **Lennoxlove House** dates from the 14th century and is home to the Duke of Hamilton. There is a collection of Mary, Queen of Scots memorabilia and fine furniture,

paintings and porcelain. Also gardens and a café run by Clarissa Dickson-Wright of *Two Fat Ladies* television fame. Open Easter to September, Wednesday, Saturday and Sunday 1400–1630. Charge for admission to house only. Telephone (01620) 823720. **St Mary's Collegiate Church** is a magnificent 14th-century medieval cruciform church, partly destroyed during the siege of 1548 and completely restored in the early 1970s. Gift and book shop and picnic area. Open April to September, Monday– Saturday 1100–1600, Sunday 0930–1230 and 1400–1630. Admission free. Telephone (01620) 823109. Next door to the church is **St Mary's Pleasance**, a labelled collection of herbs and medicinal plants, brought together 'for the enjoyment of the public'. Good picnic spot. The **Jane Welsh Carlyle Museum**, Lodge Street, is located in her now restored childhood home. In 1821 she met and was courted by Thomas Carlyle, the writer and philosopher. Lovely garden and a good place to picnic. Open April to September, Wednesday–Saturday 1400– 1700. Admission charge for house, garden free. Telephone (01620) 823738.

Ⓒ Seton Collegiate Church, near Port Seton

The chancel and apse of a fine 15th-century church with 16th-century transept and steeple, in a beautiful walled area with lawns and peacocks. Historic Scotland property. Open April to September, Monday–Saturday 0930– 1830, Sunday 1400–1830. Charge. Telephone (01875) 813334.

Ⓓ Prestongrange Industrial Heritage Museum, Prestonpans

A museum telling the story of many local industries. Displays include a Cornish beam engine. Visitor centre, café (open weekends only) and picnic area. Open April to October, daily 1100–1600. Admission free. Telephone 0131 653 2904.

Food and drink

Plenty of choice in Musselburgh, pubs and cafés in Haddington and a café in Port Seton. There is a farm shop on the road between Seton Church and Port Seton. Refreshments are also available at Lennoxlove House and Preston-grange Museum.

☕ **Ipa Nema, Musselburgh**
Serves the usual café fare.

🍺 **The Carlyle, Haddington**
Popular with cyclists.

☕ **Golden Grain, Haddington**
Lunch, afternoon tea and high tea served.

☕ **Harbour Café, Port Seton**
Snacks served all day.

Route description

Start at Musselburgh Town Hall in the High Street. Take Newbigging Road (opposite the town hall) for 300m, SP Inveresk. TR at TJ, SP Inveresk, and immediately TL up hill, SP Inveresk.

1   TL as road goes left. Pass Inveresk Lodge Garden on right, TL into Crookston Road and eventually SO through bollards.

2   Cycle path ends. Continue along cul-de-sac and TR to cross bridge over the A1, no SP. TL into minor road, no SP, and pass Crookston Farm for a long, steep climb.

3   SO onto track at top of hill as road turns sharp left, SP Elphinstone. SO at crossing of tracks, past bollard. SO where track divides at second bollards – re-cycled industrial gas bottles, upended! (6km/3.5 miles). Continue as track becomes farm track. Views back of Falside Castle and ahead of Traprain Law, Haddington, North Berwick Law and the tip of Bass Rock.

4 Track ends. Cross B road and SO on minor road, SP Research Centre. TR at TJ, no SP. Then, TL at TJ, no SP (bus shelter and SP Buxley opposite).

5 TR at TJ onto B6355 for 50m, no SP. TL onto track, SP Penston and New Winton. Continue SO past barrier (9.5km/6 miles), and SO past second barrier onto farm track to Penston Farm.

6 TR onto B6363, no SP, and head towards Lammermuir Hills for 1km (0.6 mile).

7 Easy to miss – TL at TJ onto minor road, no SP but where road bends slightly to right. SO at XR along wooded road, no SP.

8 TL at TJ onto A6093, no SP. TR at XR, SP Samuelston, and continue down hill through pretty hamlet. Cross bridge over Tyne Water and immediately:

9 TR (effectively SO) at TJ for 300m, no SP. Bear left (effectively SO) at TJ by Begbie Farm, no SP. **17.5km (11 miles)**

10 TL at TJ, no SP (but note old SP in furlongs pointing back to Begbie). Enter Bolton (church has benches at rear, with delightful view through trees across stream). Continue through village and TR at TJ onto minor road, no SP but where road bends left at foot of hill.

11 TL onto track, SP Lennoxlove Estate Office, and continue to Lennoxlove House. Benches and grassy areas here. Leave House by main tarmacked entrance. Continue for 1km (0.6 mile) to road, where TL, no SP.

12 TR at TJ, SP Haddington. Cross Tyne Water (riverside walk on right, with benches). Pass St Mary's Church and TR into St Mary's Pleasance. Keep right through garden, along tunnel of laburnum, through gateway into churchyard where keep left, through another gateway to riverside. TL, towards bridge. Continue SO past Holy Trinity Church into Church Street. **29km (18 miles)**

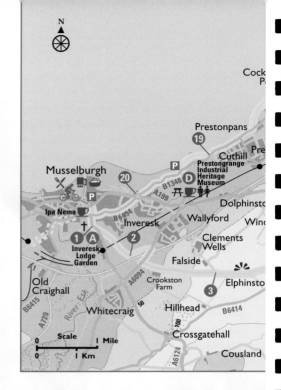

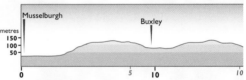

13 SO at XR into High Street. The George Hotel, on opposite corner, displays the old CTC Winged Wheel emblem. Pass Lodge Street (small cobbled road), location of Jane Welsh Carlyle's House. TR at XR (traffic lights), SP Aberlady.

14 SO at roundabout, SP Aberlady A6137. Steady climb. TL at TJ at top of hill, SP Coates.

15 RHF as road forks among trees, no SP. View ahead up Forth Estuary to Forth Bridge, the Ochil Hills, Arthur's Seat, the Pentland and Moorfoot Hills. TR at TJ, no SP, and continue through Coates.

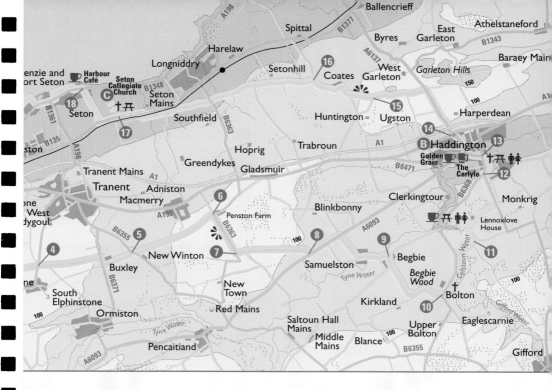

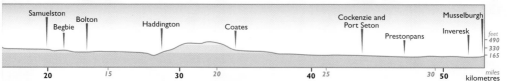

16 Easy to miss – TL at TJ, SP Railway Walk. Continue SO at all junctions until road runs close to railway (main line). TR at level crossing (St Germain's), and immediately TL onto A198 (use cycle lane on this busy road).

17 To visit Seton Collegiate Church, TR at TJ, SP Seton Collegiate Church. Follow track through trees to church (picnic spot). Otherwise, continue and TR at TJ onto minor road, SP Port Seton.

18 TL at TJ into main road, no SP, and enter Port Seton. TR at Harbour Café, SP East Coast Trail, and follow track round past Port Seton harbour into High Street. Rejoin main road.

TR onto tarmac path on seaward side of Cockenzie Power Station. Depending on the tide, you can continue along the seafront from the power station through Prestonpans. At some point, return to main road (plenty of access points).

19 Arrive end of houses at far end of Prestonpans. TR onto short track towards sea and join tarmac path over dunes, ending in car park. Rejoin road, opposite Preston Grange Industrial Heritage Museum.

20 SO at roundabout, SP Inveresk B6414. TR into Newbigging (opposite car salesroom) and return to Town Hall to complete the route.

53km (33 miles)

THE YARROW AND ETTRICK VALLEYS

Route information

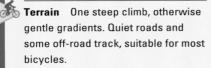

 Distance   54km (33.5 miles)

 Grade   Moderate

Terrain   One steep climb, otherwise gentle gradients. Quiet roads and some off-road track, suitable for most bicycles.

 Time to allow   5 hours.

Getting there by car   Broadmeadows Youth Hostel is at Yarrowford, 8km (5 miles) south west of Selkirk on the A708 Moffat road. Park at the hostel or in roadside car park in Yarrowford.

Getting there by train   There is no practical railway access to this ride. However, buses from Edinburgh to Selkirk will carry bicycles. Telephone Lowland buses on 0131 663 1945 for information. To reach the route from Selkirk, take the A708, heading south. Continue on this road for 3km (2 miles) and join route at direction 9, where continue SO to Yarrowford and follow the route from its start.

From Yarrowford the route climbs gently up the Yarrow valley to St Mary's Loch, and on to the far end of the loch to historic Tibbie Shiel's Inn. On, up a steep off-road track into forest for a long descent into the Ettrick valley and thence back to Yarrowford. The scenery on this route is unsurpassed and the roads used carry very little traffic.

Places of interest along the route

Ⓐ Broadmeadows Youth Hostel

This is Scotland's oldest youth hostel and is situated high above the Yarrow Water. It is a simple-grade hostel, which has been modernised only by adding basic facilities. The footpath access, separate from that for vehicles, is an adventure in itself. Telephone (01750) 76262 for further information.

Ⓑ Yarrow Kirk, Yarrow

The original church was first built in the 12th century, high on the hillside overlooking St Mary's Loch. In 1640 a new church was erected at Kirkstead and extended in the 18th, 19th and 20th centuries. In 1922 a fire completely destroyed the building, which was rebuilt as close to the previous design as possible. Sir Walter Scott worshipped here at times, and his maternal grandfather was minister between 1691 and 1710. Access at all reasonable times. Admission by donation.

Ⓒ St Mary's Loch

Beautifully set among smooth green hills, this 4.5km (3 mile) long loch is used for sailing and fishing. On the neck of land separating it from Loch of the Lowes, at the south end, stands

Tibbie Shiel's Inn. The inn was kept by Tibbie Shiel (Elizabeth Richardson, 1783–1878) from 1823 and was a meeting place for many 19th-century writers. Beside the road towards the north end of the loch is a seated statue of James Hogg, the Ettrick Shepherd, author of *Confessions of a Justified Sinner* and a friend of Scott, who farmed in this district.

Ⓓ Aikwood Tower, Selkirk

A 16th-century tower house restored in the 1990s by the Steel family to a standard that has resulted in many architectural awards. It houses a permanent exhibition relating to the life and work of James Hogg, the Ettrick Shepherd, and temporary exhibitions of art and sculpture. Open April to September, Tuesday, Thursday and Sunday 1400–1700. Charge. Telephone (01750) 52253.

Ⓔ Bowhill House and Country Park, Bowhill

Bowhill, the home of the Scotts of Buccleuch, contains an outstanding collection of pictures, including works by Van Dyck, Reynolds, Gainsborough, Canaletto and Raeburn. There is also a selection of the world-famous Buccleuch collection of portrait miniatures, porcelain, furniture and a restored Victorian kitchen. The country park has a visitor centre, woodland area, garden nature trails and bicycles for hire. Gift shop, tearoom and picnic

Food and drink

Refreshments are available at Bowhill Country Park.

Ⓓ **Gordon Arms Hotel, Yarrow**
Tea and coffee served all day, lunches between 1200–1400. Picnic tables and benches outside. Also bunkhouse accommodation.

Ⓓ **Tibbie Shiel's Inn, St Mary's Loch**
Bar meals, lunch and high tea served.

Ⓒ **Glen Café, near St Mary's Loch**
Picnic tables and benches outside. Drinks and snacks available.

Ⓓ **Tushielaw Inn, Tushielaw**
Meals served in the evenings at weekends (1km/0.6 mile off the route).

Ⓓ **Cross Keys, Ettrickbridge**
Pub serving morning coffee and bar meals.

area. House and park open July 1300–1630; park only open May–August, Saturday–Thursday 1200–1700. Charge. Telephone (01750) 22204.

Route description

Start at Yarrowford on the A708, below Broadmeadows Youth Hostel. TR from hostel exit, heading towards Moffat and follow road through valley.

1 Pass Yarrow Kirk on right. *6.5km (4 miles)*

2 SO at XR by Gordon Arms, SP Moffat (13km/8 miles). Continue on A708, alongside St Mary's Loch to south end.

3 TL at TJ, SP Tibbie Shiel's.

4 Bear left near entrance to pub, SP Southern Upland Way. Continue SO through gate onto track, SP Vehicles use at own risk. Climb steeply. Views back over loch. Cross cattle grid and SO on main track, ignoring Southern Upland Way going to right. Continue on track, through forest.

5 Track ends. View of Yarrow valley to left. TR onto B709 and descend. *27.5km (17 miles)*

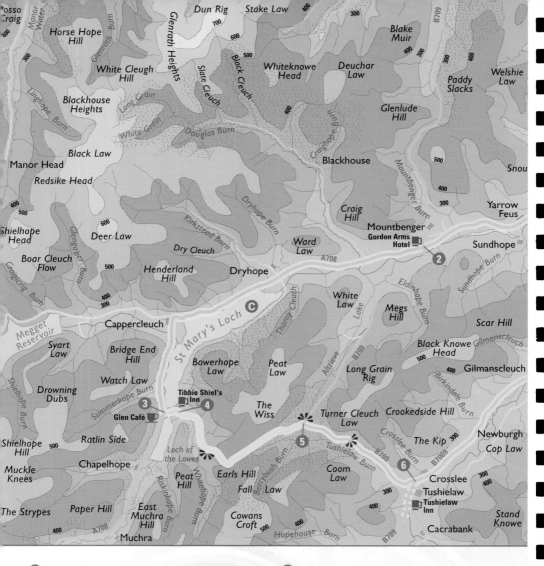

6 To visit Tushielaw Inn, TR for 1km/0.6 mile. To continue route, TL at TJ, SP Selkirk B7009 (31.5km/19.5 miles). Continue on this road, through Ettrickbridge (42.5km/26.5 miles), SO at all junctions.

7 To visit Aikwood Tower, TR SP Aikwood Tower. Otherwise, continue SO.

42.5km (26.5 miles)

8 TL at TJ, SP Yarrow valley B7009 (49km/30.5 miles). Pass entrance to Bowhill House and Country Park.

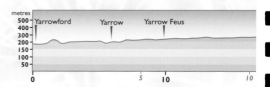

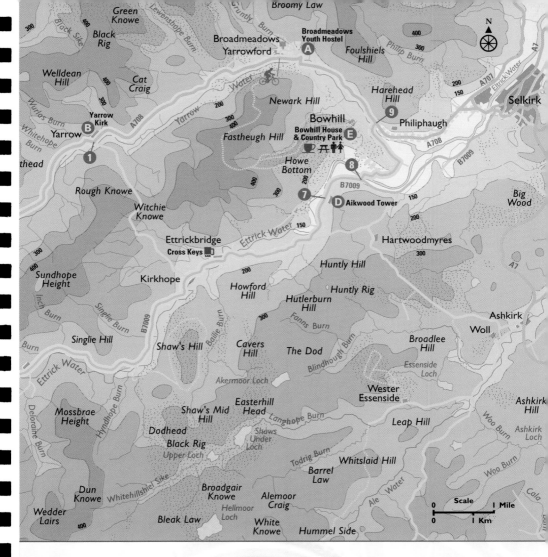

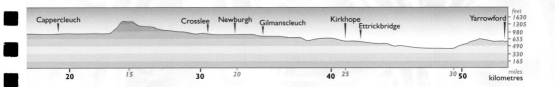

9 TL at TJ, SP A708 Moffat. Follow A708 back to Yarrowford to complete the route.

54km (33.5miles)

If started route from Selkirk, TR onto A708, SP Selkirk, and cycle 3km (2 miles) back to Selkirk to complete the route.

Route 17

EAST LOTHIAN – DUNBAR TO HADDINGTON

Route information

Distance   55km (34 miles)

Grade   Strenuous

Terrain   The route crosses a number of ravines in the foothills of the Lammermuir Hills. There are no major climbs, but the hills are surprisingly tough. The return route is over much gentler ground. Mostly minor roads and two short off-road sections, suitable for most bicycles with gears to cope with the hills.

Time to allow   5–6 hours.

Getting there by car   Dunbar is 50km (31 miles) north east of Edinburgh, just off the A1. Car parking is available at the station at the south end of Dunbar. Follow SP for Town Centre, TR into High Street and follow one-way system to the station.

Getting there by train   There is a railway station at Dunbar, served by trains from Edinburgh. Telephone (0345) 484950 for information.

This route covers some beautiful East Lothian countryside, travelling through picturesque and historic villages, and is almost entirely on quiet roads. Some villages, such as Garvald, tucked away in the hills, have a feeling of remoteness and isolation despite being only a few miles from Dunbar. The roads are often wooded, giving shelter, and there is a ford to splash through.

Places of interest along the route

A **Dunbar**

The fishing port of Dunbar was a royal burgh from 1445 and was attacked twice by the Earl of Hertford in the 16th century. **Dunbar Town House Museum**, High Street, displays information on local history and archaeology. Open April to October, daily 1230–1630. Admission free. Telephone (01368) 863734. Dunbar was the birthplace of John Muir, the founding figure of the worldwide conservation movement. In **John Muir House** visitors can examine the flat furnished as it would have been when Muir lived there. An audio-visual display tells his story. Open June to September, Monday–Saturday 1100–1300 and 1400–1700, Sunday 1400–1700. Admission free. Telephone (01368) 862585. **Dunbar Church** was rebuilt after a disastrous fire in 1987. It has a modern interior with bright stained glass, and a marble and alabaster monument to the Earl of Dunbar, which has stood in churches on this site since the early 17th century. Gift shop. Tea and coffee available. Open June to September, Monday–Saturday 1100–1600, Sunday 1400–1600. Admission by donation. Telephone Dunbar Tourist Information Centre on (01368) 863353 for further information.

B **Haddington**

Once a royal burgh, Haddington was destroyed three times by the English during the 13th century border wars and again during the 14th century. The town also survived a 16-month long siege whilst it was occupied by the English in 1548–9. For further information, see route 15.

C Preston Mill and Phantassie Doocot

Set in a charming location with ducks and geese on the millponds, this picturesque mill and stone building dates from the 18th century. The water wheel and grain milling machinery are intact and visitors can see them in operation. The 16th-century doocot was once home to 500 pigeons. National Trust for Scotland property. Gift shop. Open Easter and May to September, Monday–Saturday 1100–1300 and 1400–1700, Sunday 1330–1700; October, weekends only 1330–1600. Charge. Telephone (01620) 860426.

D John Muir Country Park, Tyninghame

Covering an area of 733ha (1760 acres) and established in 1976, the park has three sites, two on the outskirts of Dunbar and one near Tyning-hame. The latter is the nicest. There is a fine sandy beach, woodland, rocky headlands, dunes, and views of Bass Rock.

Food and drink

There are cafés, pubs, take-aways and convenience stores in Dunbar. Plenty of choice in Haddington and East Linton, where there are also convenience stores.

Leisure Pool Cafeteria, High Street, Dunbar
Recommended for good value snacks.

The Starfish, Old Harbour, Dunbar
Bar lunches served in picturesque surroundings.

The Gallery, Stenton
Coffee available.

Garvald Hotel, Garvald
Bar lunches offered.

Drovers Inn, East Linton
Coffee and bar meals served.

Coffee Shop, Tyninghame
Tea, coffee and lunches available.

Route description

From Dunbar Station TL into Station Road, then TR following one-way system. TR again then SO, SP Berwick-upon-Tweed. TR at TJ into minor road, SP Spott. Continue for 1km (0.6 mile).

1 SO across A1 (with care) at staggered XR, SP Spott. Climb steadily to Spott and SO through village. *4km (2.5 miles)*

2 Easy to miss – TR at TJ onto very minor road, no SP (but SP for Ford and Bends for 1m). Descend and cross ford. Climb and descend to foot of hill where:

3 TL at TJ, no SP.

4 At hamlet of Pitcox, SO at XR, SP Stenton B6370. Follow this road to Stenton.

5 Arrive Stenton (at edge of village look out for half-hidden 16th-century well on right). In centre of village a notice board describes the interesting buildings (10km/6 miles). Leave village. Road becomes wooded as you descend, climb and descend again – loose gravel on bends, take care.

6 Easy to miss – TL at TJ at foot of hill, as road starts to rise, SP Garvald (B6370). Climb again.

7 TL at TJ, SP East Lothian Hillfoot Trail, for another steep descent. TR sharply at foot of hill, pass church and enter Garvald where TR at TJ, SP Haddington. *(17km/10.5 miles)*

8 TR at TJ at end of village, SP Haddington. Then TL at TJ, SP Haddington, and TR at TJ, SP Haddington.

9 TL at Morham TJ, SP Haddington, for long steady descent through wood. *21.5km (13.5 miles)*

10 TR at TJ onto B6369, no SP, for 200m. TR (effectively SO) at TJ (where B6369 goes left), SP Nungate, for short climb. Continue SO at all junctions to Haddington.

11 To visit Haddington, SO at XR. Otherwise, to continue route, TR at XR (following main road), SP Hailes Castle.
26.5km (16.5 miles)

12 TR opposite golf course entrance. Continue.

13 TR at TJ, SP Garvald and continue on this road for 3km (2 miles).
28.5km (17.5 miles)

14 TL at XR, old SP Garvald SO (31.5km (19.5 miles). Continue on this road to Luggate.

15 Arrive Luggate. TL at TJ (effectively SO), SP East Linton. Then, TL at TJ, SP East Linton. Climb past Traprain Farm (36.5km/22.5 miles). Steep descent to:

16 SO across A1 (with care) at XR, SP East Linton. To visit East Linton, TL at TJ, no SP. Cross River Tyne. TR at TJ, SP Preston Mill (38km/23.5 miles). Otherwise, TR at TJ.

17 TL onto track opposite filling station for 100m, SP Houston Mill. TR and follow track around farm outbuildings. Track becomes tarmac. Pass Phantassie Doocot on right. Continue SO on track, across footbridge, through gate, across field and through second gate to reach Preston Mill. Leave Mill by main exit and TR onto B1407. Continue on this road to Tyninghame.

18 Arrive Tyninghame. To continue route, TR at TJ onto A198 and continue to A1 and direction 19. To visit John Muir Country Park, TL at TJ onto A198 for 1km (0.6 mile), SP North Berwick.
41.5km (26 miles)

a TR at TJ onto minor road (known as Limetree Walk), no SP but opposite forest gate. Continue on road for 2km (1 mile) to car park where SO past barrier onto track in woods.

b Bear left on track to sandy beach, dunes,

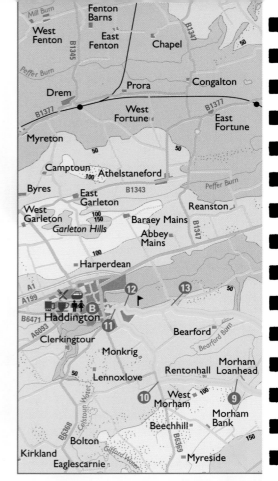

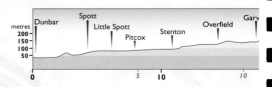

headland and good views. The track SO leads to a beach with views across Tyninghame Bay to Belhaven and Dunbar, and picnic area. Both beaches worth visiting. Retrace route along Limetree Walk to A198 where TL. Continue SO through Tyninghame to reach A1, which has a cycle path along its north side.

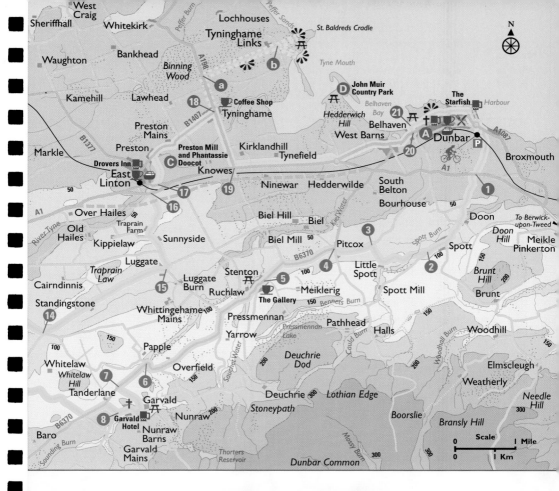

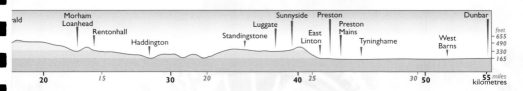

19 Arrive A1 and TL onto cycle path. Continue as cycle path joins A1087, SP Dunbar (51.5km/32 miles). Pass caravan park.

20 TL into Shore Road, SP John Muir CP. Follow road to beach (picnic spot). Retrace route as far as Back Road.

21 TL onto Back Road and climb into Dunbar. Views of Bass Rock, North Berwick Law and spectacular rock formations. Follow road around into High Street and continue to station to complete the route.

55km (34 miles)

PENICUIK, THE MELDON HILLS AND WEST LINTON

Route information

Distance 58km (36 miles)

Grade Moderate

Terrain The route mainly follows valleys. There are a number of climbs but they are all fairly gentle and evenly graded. The optional 8km (5 mile) loop to Kirkton Manor includes some off-road cycling, suitable for most bicycles.

Time to allow 5 hours.

Getting there by car Penicuik is 18km (11 miles) south of Edinburgh on the A701. Park in the Safeway supermarket car park off the A701 in Penicuik.

Getting there by train The nearest railway station is Edinburgh Waverley, 18km (11 miles) away. TL out of the station onto Waverley Bridge. SO at XR (roundabout) up Cockburn Street (steep – you might want to walk). TL into High Street and TR (with care) at XR into South Bridge. This is the A701 which you follow all the way into Penicuik. It has short sections of cycle lane, separate cycle track and protected lane.

This route takes you from Midlothian into the Borders. From Penicuik you head south to the Tweed valley, along a scenic road through the Meldon Hills. This area is a favourite destination for Sunday outings, with beautiful scenery and a pretty stream. The Tweed valley has lovely landscape of rolling hills, woods and farmland. The optional loop to Kirkton Manor takes in some of the best of this. En route there is a good view of the Neidpath Viaduct, opened in 1864 for what eventually became the Caledonian Railway. Each of its eight arches were built on a skew as the line curved from left to right across the Tweed. The return route follows the Lyne Water, from its junction with the Tweed to its head waters at West Linton, and then crosses Auchencorth Moss, a fast and exhilarating ride if the prevailing south west wind is blowing.

Places of interest along the route

A **Penicuik**

Once well-known for its papermills (the last closed in 1975), Penicuik has developed from a small village into a sizeable town. Penicuik House, built in 1761, was largely destroyed by fire in 1899 and only a shell stands on the Estate today. **Edinburgh Crystal Visitor Centre** is sign-posted on the left on the way into Penicuik from

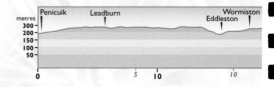

Food and drink

Plenty of choice in Penicuik – the eating places are all close to each other towards the south end of town. Also cafés and pubs and a convenience store in West Linton.

Peni Deli, Penicuik
One of the best choices for refreshment in town.

Olympia Café, Penicuik
Good choice for Italian ice cream.

Leadburn Inn, Leadburn
The pub has a restaurant in an old railway coach in the garden.

Scots Pine Restaurant, Eddleston
Lunches and evening meals offered.

Romano Inn, Romannobridge
Lots of old farm implements on outside wall. Bar lunches served.

Gallery Tearoom, West Linton
Tea and coffee served in art gallery.

Edinburgh, before the junction of the A701 and A766. Visitors can tour the factory and see glass products being made and engraved. Coffee shop and picnic area. Open all year, Monday–Saturday 0900–1700, Sunday 1100–1700. Admission free. Charge for factory tour. Telephone (01968) 675128.

B West Linton

There has been a settlement here since at least the 12th century. The village was on the main drovers route and at one time was known for its sheep fairs, some of the largest in Scotland. Lady Gifford Statue, on the front of the village clock, was carved in 1666 by James Gifford, a Covenanter and skilled stonemason. The clock is on the site of a well, disused since Victorian times. James Gifford also executed panels (1660 and 1678) on a house opposite, depicting Lady Gifford and the entire family genealogy.

Route description

TR out of the Safeway car park and head south on A701, SP Peebles. Descend to cross River North Esk and pass Penicuik South Kirk on right. Continue on A701 for steady climb to Leadburn. Views to right and behind of Pentland Hills.

1 SO at Leadburn XR, SP Peebles A703 (5km/3 miles). Stay on A703 over Leadburn summit. It is downhill or level from here to Eddleston. Views of Moorfoot Hills ahead and left.

2 TL by Scots Pine restaurant. Follow old road to Eddleston. ***13km (8 miles)***

3 Arrive Eddleston (picnic places here). TR at TJ, SP Lyne via Meldons. Climb steadily with

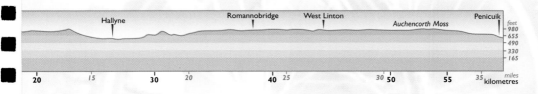

excellent views along valley to Peebles and the hills beyond. Summit is reached at 17km (10.5 miles), followed by long gentle descent on unfenced road – beware wandering sheep. Pass parking place, with picnic tables and WC beside pretty stream. *15km (9.5 miles)*

4 LHF at junction, no SP.

5 Arrive TJ with A72. To bypass Kirkton Loop, TR and follow A72 to direction 6. Otherwise, TL, SP Peebles. Pass Lyne Station, where railway and old road cross Lyne Water, as it joins the Tweed.

Penicuik Estate

a TR at TJ, SP Kirkton Manor (24km/ 15 miles). Continue for steady climb – the road is sheltered by woods and an avenue of beeches. Excellent views of Tweed Valley.

b Arrive Kirkton Manor. Easy to miss – TR, through white gate at lodge house, onto track (before church and phone box). Pass farm with octagonal tower on left and ruined keep on right. Keep SO, SP Tweed Walk.
27.5km (17 miles)

c SO at TJ at gateposts for 200m, on narrow track past cottages on right, small SP Tweed Walk. LHF onto footpath, SP Tweed Cycleway. Cross footbridge and continue on track to Lyne Station where TR at TJ, SP Weak Bridge. Cross Lyne Water. TL at TJ onto A72, no SP. Continue along A72 to Ladykirk.

6 TR at TJ, SP West Linton B7059 (33km/ 20.5 miles). Cross the Lyne Water and continue to Romannobridge.

7 TL opposite Romano Inn. Cross the Lyne Water by old bridge and join A701.

8 TR at TJ, SP Bogsbank (41km/25.5 miles). Steady climb with view of Pentlands ahead. Continue on this road to West Linton

9 LHF at TJ and cross the Lyne Water for last time. Enter West Linton. Cycle through village, passing Lady Gifford Statue.

10 TR at TJ into Deanfoot Road, no SP (opposite Linton Hotel).

11 SO at XR, SP Penicuik (49.5km/31 miles). Continue on this road over Auchencorth Moss.

12 LHF at TJ onto A701 (56km/35 miles). Follow this road back into Penicuik. TL into the Safeway car park to complete the route.
58km (36 miles)

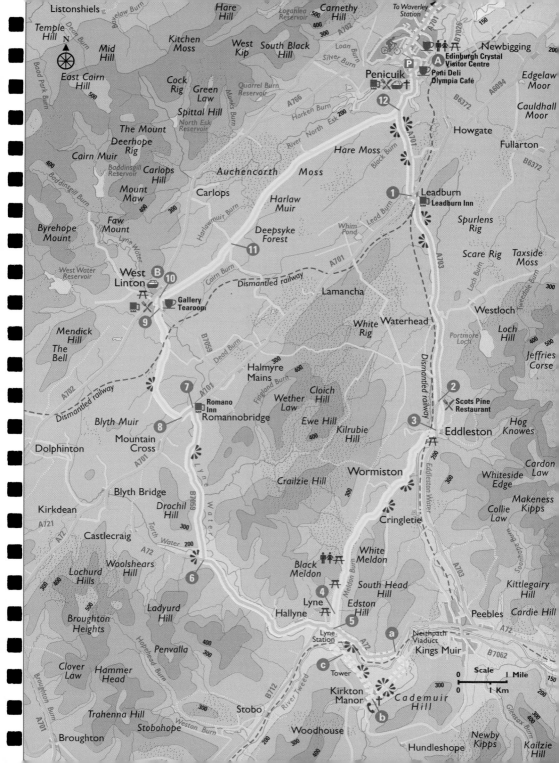

NORTH BERWICK

Route information

 Distance   61km (38 miles)

Grade   Moderate

Terrain   Quite hilly in parts, with climbs out of North Berwick and Haddington. The return is relatively flat. Virtually traffic-free roads.

Time to allow   5 hours.

Getting there by car   North Berwick is on the coast, 36km (22.5 miles) north west of Edinburgh, north of the A1 on the A198. There is a car park at the railway station.

Getting there by train   There is a railway station at North Berwick served by trains from Edinburgh. Bicycles carried free. Telephone (0345) 484950 for information.

This route takes in spectacular coastal scenery beyond North Berwick, passing Tantallon Castle and the Bass Rock. Turning inland, the countryside is hilly and well wooded, becoming more open between Biel and Haddington. The return takes you through the picturesque villages of Athelstaneford, Drem and Dirleton, and the nature reserve and beach at Yellowcraig.

Bass Rock and Tantallon Castle

Places of interest along the route

Ⓐ **North Berwick**
There has been a settlement here for thousands of years. The town was a prosperous fishing and trading port but is now a popular holiday resort. **North Berwick Museum**, in School Road, has a wide range of fascinating displays on local history. Gift shop. Open April to October, daily 1100–1700. Admission free. Telephone (01620) 895457. The **Bass Rock**, once used as a prison, today a wildlife sanctuary, lies 4.5km (3 miles) off North Berwick.

Ⓑ Tantallon Castle, near North Berwick

The remains of a remarkable fortification with earthwork defences and a massive 14th-century curtain wall with towers. Historic Scotland property. Gift shop and tearoom. Open April to September, Monday–Saturday 0930–1830, Sunday 1400–1830; October to March, Monday–Saturday 0930–1830, Sunday 1400–1630 (closed Thursday afternoon and Friday). Charge. Telephone (01620) 892727.

Ⓒ Hailes Castle, near East Linton

Castle ruins in a beautiful location. Historic Scotland property. Picnic area. Access at all reasonable times. Free. Telephone 0131 668 8800.

Ⓓ Haddington

Once a royal burgh, Haddington was destroyed three times by the English during the 13th-century border wars and again during the 14th century. See route 15 for further information.

Ⓔ Athelstaneford Heritage Centre

An 11th-century doocot, restored to house an unmanned audio-visual display on the origins of the Saltire – Scotland's national flag. Nice picnic spot. Open at all reasonable times. Admission free. Telephone (01620) 880378.

Ⓕ Museum of Flight, East Fortune Airfield

Scotland's national museum of aviation. Gift shop, tearoom and garden. Open April to October, daily 1030–1700; November to March, weekends only 1100–1500. Charge (admission free in winter). Telephone (01620) 880308.

Ⓖ Dirleton Castle and Gardens, Dirleton

Romantic 13th-century castle, with 15th- and 17th-century additions. Historic Scotland property. Gift shop. Open April to September, Monday–Saturday 0930–1830, Sunday 1400–1830; October to March, Monday–Saturday 0930–1630, Sunday 1400–1630. Charge. Telephone (01620) 850330.

Route description

TL out of North Berwick Station. Then TR and follow one-way system to far end of sea front. To visit harbour, TL at TJ. Otherwise, TR into Quality Street. TL at War Memorial (opposite Tourist Information Centre) and follow main road up hill, with golf links and tennis courts on left.

1 TL onto A198 and continue SO at all junctions to Tantallon Castle. Spectacular views of North Berwick Law, the rocky coast, sandy beaches and, out to sea, the Bass Rock and the Isle of May.

2 TR where main road turns sharp left, SP Blackdykes. **6km (3.5 miles)**

3 TL at TJ, no SP. Pass Blackdykes Farm. Look out for potholes on next sharp left hand corner.

4 TL at TJ, SP Dunbar (11km/7 miles). Views from summit ahead of Traprain Law and, in the distance, Torness Power Station. Continue, following road as it bears sharp left and then sharp right.

5 TR (effectively SO) at TJ, no SP (after road bends sharp right, as main road goes left). TL at TJ, no SP. Then TR at TJ, SP East Linton. Note that someone has converted nearly every East Linton SP to Fast Linton! Steep descent.

6 TL at TJ beside farm, SP Lawhead. Good views from summit after farm.

7 TR at TJ onto A198, no SP. Long descent through Tyninghame (coffee shop SP right). Cross River Tyne and continue.

8 Cross A1 with care (use central refuge) and TR for 20m. TL by house and cross footbridge over railway. Follow road uphill through trees. **19.5km (12 miles)**

9 TR at XR, no SP (but TL SP Biel). SO at XR, SP Luggate.

10 TR at TJ at Luggate, SP East Linton.

11 TL into minor road at TJ on crest of hill by farm, SP Kippielaw. Continue for several steep descents with sharp bends – take care. View ahead of Tyne Valley and East Linton. TL at TJ, no SP. Pass Hailes Castle and continue. **26.5km (16.5 miles)**

12 TR at TJ, SP Haddington. Continue SO at all junctions, SP Haddington, until reach golf course gateway entrance where TL, SP Haddington.

13 TR as road bends left, SP Town Centre. Then, bear left into Bridge Street and cross Nungate Bridge. TR into Church Street, SP Town Centre. **33km (20.5 miles)**

14 TR at XR then SO at traffic lights into Hardgate.

15 At this and next roundabout, follow SP Drem for long climb. Views from summit to east and north. Then, steep descent.

16 Easy to miss – TR onto B1343 at TJ at foot of hill, SP Athelstaneford. **36km (22.5 miles)**

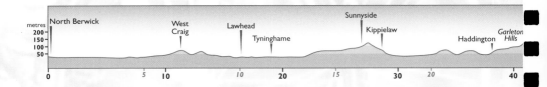

Fidra

Lamb

Craigleith

Bass Rock

N

Brigs of Fidra

Longskelly Pt

North Berwick

The Leithies

Yellowcraig Beach

Broad Sands

A198

Milsey Bay

Rugged Knowes

Canty Bay

St Baldreds Boat

A

George Café

P

i

1

North Berwick Law

Car Rocks

B Tantallon Castle

Auldhame

22

Ferrygate

Newhouse

Blackdykes Farm

3

2

Scorighall

21

Dirleton

G Dirleton Castle and Gardens

Highfield

Wamphray

Pilmuir

Burn

Glaghornie

Peffer Sands

Kingston

Balgane

4

Redside East Craig

New Mains

Pefferside

West Craig

5

50

Lochhouses

Fenton Barns Village Coffee Shop

20

Chapel

Brownfrog

Bankhead

Stonelaws

Whitekirk

Tyninghame Links

West Fenton

B1345

Muirton

B1341

Waughton

Congalton

Newbyth

Binning Wood

A198

River Tyne

Mill Burn

Peffer Burn

Drem

Prora

West Fortune

B1377

Kamehill

Lawhead

Tyninghame

B1377

Myreton

East Fortune Airfield

Preston Mains

Farm

6 Coffee Shop

7

Camptoun

Athelstaneford Heritage Centre

19

F Museum of Flight

Peffer Burn

B1377

Markle

B1407

Preston

Farm Shop

To Dunbar

A1

East Garleton

B1343

17 † **E**

18

East Linton

Knowes

8

Ninewar

Athelstaneford

Reanston

Hownuir

16 Garleton Hills

100

150

Abbey Mains

B1347

A1

Over Hailes

Hailes Castle **C**

Sunnyside

11

Biel Hill

9

50

B6370

Alderston Mains

100

15

River Tyne

Kippielaw

10

Luggate

Luggate Burn

Stenton

100

Alderston

Cairndinnis

Traprain Law

Whittingehame Mains

Ruchlaw

150

A1

D

Haddington

12

Pressmennan Lake

150 200

B6471

14 **13**

Bearford

Bearford Burn

50

100

Yarrow

Woodend

A6093

Clerkingtour

B6368

B6369

Scale

0 ——— 1 Mile

0 ——— 1 Km

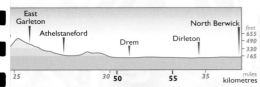

17 Arrive Athelstaneford. Pass Heritage Centre, church and Saltire Monument on left. SO at TJ, SP East Linton (main road goes left). Views of North Berwick Law on left, Traprain Law on right. Then TL at TJ, SP East Fortune (this SP has been converted to Fast Fortune).

18 To visit Museum of Flight, SO at junction and museum entrance is on right. Otherwise, TL.

19 TR at TJ, SP East Fortune Hospital, then TL at TJ, SP Drem. Continue towards Drem and over railway bridge. TR at TJ onto

B1345, into Drem. Follow road, SP Fenton Barns.

20 Pass slip road to Fenton Barns on right.

21 TR then immediate TL at staggered XR with A198, SP Dirleton. Enter village and pass Dirleton Castle on right.   *51.5km (32 miles)*

22 To visit Yellowcraig beach and nature reserve, TL at TJ, SP Yellowcraig. Otherwise, continue SO on A198 back into North Berwick. The railway station and the end of the route is on the right.   *61km (38 miles)*

North Berwick

Food and drink

Lots of choice in North Berwick and Haddington, with cafés, pubs and take-aways. Also farm shop at Knowes and tearooms at Tantallon Castle and the Museum of Flight.

George Café, High Street, North Berwick
Popular with cyclists.

Coffee Shop, Tyninghame
Drinks and snacks. Just off main road towards East Linton.

The Carlyle, Haddington
Popular with cyclists.

Golden Grain, Haddington
Lunch, afternoon and high tea.

Village Coffee Shop, Fenton Barns
Tea, coffee and light meals. Not open Thursday. Also picnic spot.

Route information

Distance   63km (39 miles)

Grade   Moderate

Terrain   Minor roads with a short off-road section. The outward route has some moderate hills, the return is rather undulating. Suitable for most bicycles.

Time to allow   6–7 hours.

Getting there by car   Biggar is 48km (30 miles) south west of Edinburgh, on the A702. Car parking is available on the main street in the centre of town.

Getting there by train   There is no practical railway access to this ride.

Using the Tweed Cycleway, the route starts from Biggar and follows the Biggar Water to Broughton and then the River Tweed to Peebles. The return is on different roads, along the same route, passing Stobo Kirk, a pleasant picnic stop. The middle section of the route, between Stobo and Lyne is quite well sheltered and offers some protection against the wind.

Places of interest along the route

Ⓐ Biggar

Biggar is full of interesting places to visit. **Biggar Gasworks Museum**, High Street, a Historic Scotland property, is the only surviving example of a small town coal-gas works in Scotland. Open June to September, daily 1400–1700. Charge. Telephone (01899) 221050. **Biggar Kirk**, High Street, dates from the 16th century and contains fine examples of modern stained glass. Open daily during summer months. Admission by donation. Telephone (01899) 211050 for further information. **Gladstone Court Museum** comprises an indoor street of shops and shop windows, including a grocer, photographer, bank and telephone exchange. Gift shop. Open Easter to October, Monday–Saturday 1000–1230 and 1400–1700, Sunday 1400–1700. Charge. Telephone (01899) 221050. **Greenhill Covenanters' House**, Burnbrae, is a farmhouse, rescued in ruinous condition and rebuilt in Biggar, 16km (10 miles) from its original site. Exhibits include relics of local Covenanters, 17th-century furnishing and rare animal breeds. Gift shop. Open Easter to September, daily 1400–1700. Charge. Telephone (01899) 221050. **International Purves Puppets**, at Biggar Little Theatre, is a unique Victorian puppet theatre, set in beautiful grounds. Gift shop, tearoom and picnic area. Guided tours available. Open all year, Monday–Saturday 1000–1700; Easter to September also Sunday 1400–1700. Charge. Telephone (01899) 220631. **Moat Park Heritage Centre**, Kirkstyle, is located in a former church, adapted to display the history of the Upper Clyde and Tweed valleys, from the days of the glacier and volcano to the present. Also fine collection of embroidery. Gift shop. Open Easter to October, Monday–Saturday 1000–1700, Sunday 1400–1700. Charge. Telephone (01899) 221050.

Food and drink

Plenty of choice in Biggar and Peebles. There is a convenience store in Broughton and refreshments are available at Purves Puppets and Dawyck Botanic Garden.

Clootie Dumpling Café, Biggar
At the north end of Biggar. Popular with cyclists.

Gillespie Centre, Old Kirk, Biggar
Good value for light snacks.

Laurel Bank Café, corner of Biggar Road, Broughton
Tea, coffee and snacks offered.

Coffee Pot, Northgate, Peebles
Traditional tearoom, selling snacks and home baking.

The Keg, High Street, Peebles
Also popular with cyclists. Serves food at lunchtimes.

John Buchan Centre, Broughton
The centre tells the story of John Buchan, 1st Lord of Tweedsmuir, author of *The Thirty-Nine Steps,* and lawyer, politician, soldier, historian and Governor-General of Canada. Bookshop. Open Easter and May to September, daily 1400–1700. Charge. Telephone (01899) 221050.

Peebles
Peebles is a traditional Borders town, on the River Tweed. It used to be a centre of wool manufacture and has developed into a popular holiday resort. The **Tweeddale Museum and Gallery**, High Street, has displays of local history, craftwork, contemporary art and a gallery of ornamental plasterwork. Open March to December, Monday–Friday 1000–1200 and 1400–1700; Easter to October, also Saturday 1000–1300. Admission free. Telephone (01721) 724820. The **Cornice Museum of Ornamental Plasterwork**, Innerleithen Road, is a plasterer's casting workshop, virtually unchanged since the turn of the century. Open all year, Monday–Thursday 1030–1200 and 1400–1600, Friday 1030–1200 and 1400–1530. Admission by

Peebles

donation. Telephone (01721) 720212. **Cross Kirk**, Cross Road, is the ruin of a Trinitarian Friary founded in the 13th century. The remains include the nave, west tower and foundations of domestic buildings. Historic Scotland property. Open at all reasonable times. Telephone 0131 668 8800.

Neidpath Castle, near Peebles
Neidpath Castle is a rare example of a 14th-century castle, converted into a tower house in the 17th century. Displayed in the great hall is a beautiful batik, depicting the life of Mary, Queen of Scots. Also large collection of tartan. Good views from the parapet. Historic Scotland property. Gift shop and picnic area. Open Easter to September, Monday–Saturday 1100–1700, Sunday 1300–1700. Charge. Telephone (01721) 720333.

Dawyck Botanic Garden, Stobo
Historic arboretum with landscaped walks, part of the Royal Botanic Garden, Edinburgh. Many flowering trees, shrubs and herbaceous plants. Gift shop, tearoom and picnic area. Open March to October, daily 0930–1800. Charge. Telephone (01721) 760254.

Neidpath Castle

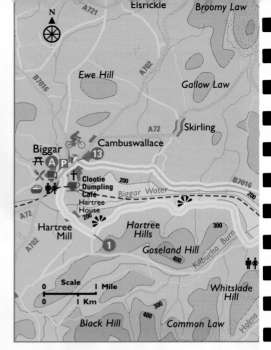

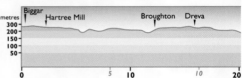

Route description

Start at the Tourist Information Centre in Biggar. Head south on the A702 for 200m. TL into Station Road, SP Tweed Cycleway. Continue on this road, sheltered by walls and trees. Pass Hartree House on left and road starts to climb, alongside hedge.

1 TL at TJ, SP Tweed Cycleway. The route now follows the Biggar Water, but at some height above it. Views on left of Tinto Hill. Continue towards Broughton.

2 TL at TJ onto A701, SP Edinburgh. This road is not usually busy, but take care.

11km (7 miles)

3 TR at TJ, no SP (Dreva Road). After crossing a stream, road climbs steeply over hill (views south up Tweed valley from summit). Long winding descent, with views of river and valley to east. Climb again to Dreva (farm and cottages), then gradually descend to valley.

4 TL at TJ onto B712, and continue through Stobo, passing kirk on left (19km/12 miles). Continue, taking RHF off B712, SP Lyne Station.

5 Arrive Lyne Station and TR at TJ, SP Tweed Cycleway. Go under old railway bridge (24km/15 miles). Road deteriorates to track and crosses footbridge over Tweed. Continue on footpath for 300m. SO through gateway onto track at TJ by cottages, SP Tweed Walk. Keep SO for 1.5km (1 mile). Exit onto road at lodge and TR into Kirkton Manor, no SP.

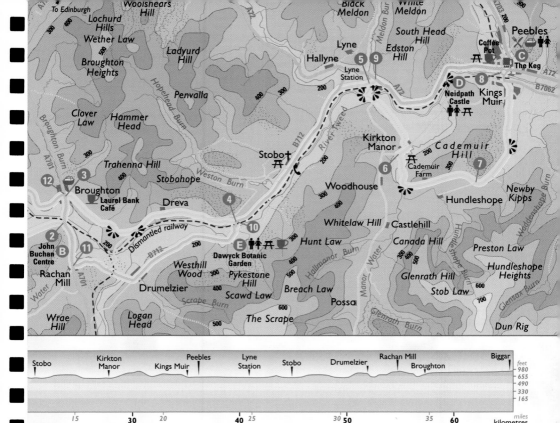

6 TL at TJ, SP Peebles via Cademuir. Cross the Manor Water (picnic spot beside river). Road climbs to summit at Cademuir Farm, then gently descends through pleasant valley.

7 Bear left at TJ, no SP (31km/19 miles). TR at TJ into Springwood Road for 200m, no SP. Then TL at TJ, SP Tweed Cycleway and bear left at TJ into Kingsmeadows Road. Cross river into Peebles.

8 To visit Peebles, TR at roundabout. Otherwise, to continue route bear left at roundabout, SP Glasgow A72 (35.5km/22 miles). Continue, passing Neidpath Castle on left.

9 TL at TJ, SP Lyne Station. Cross the Lyne Water by old bridge (40km/25 miles). Continue to B712, and retrace route along Tweed valley, through Stobo.

10 LHF (effectively SO) and continue on B712 (46.5km/29 miles). Cross River Tweed and pass Dawyck Botanic Garden. Road climbs to Drumelzier, then descends again.

11 TR at TJ, SP A701 Edinburgh (52.5km/32.5 miles). Pass John Buchan Centre on left.

12 Arrive Broughton. TL at XR in centre of village, SP Biggar B7016 (55km/34 miles). Continue on undulating road by the Biggar Water, into Biggar.

13 Arrive Biggar. TL at TJ, SP A702. The Tourist Information Centre, the end of the route, is on the right. ***63km (39 miles)***

DALKEITH, GIFFORD AND THE LAMMERMUIR HILLS

Route information

Distance   64km (40 miles)

Grade   Moderate

Terrain   The outward journey involves three climbs, and the return is mostly downhill or level. Two sections of off-road, suitable for most bicycles.

Time to allow   5–6 hours.

Getting there by car   Eskbank roundabout is at the junctions of the A768, A6094, B6392 and B703, 2km (1 mile) from Sheriffhall on the Edinburgh City Bypass. From bypass follow SP Eskbank B6392. Car parking is available in the yard of old Eskbank Station, 100m down Lasswade Road (A768).

Getting there by train   The nearest railway station is Edinburgh Waverley (11km/7 miles from Eskbank). TL out of the station onto Waverley Bridge. SO at XR (roundabout) up Cockburn Street (steep – you might want to walk). TL into High Street and TR (with care) at XR into South Bridge. This is the A701 which you follow through Newington. Then take the A772 to Eskbank.

A route of old railways, old signposts and grassy triangular junctions, through Dalkeith Country Park and along the off-road Pencaitland Path, through a peaceful valley to Pencaitland. On through some lovely East Lothian countryside and narrow minor roads to Gifford. The next section of the route takes you along the Lammermuir foothills, past some ancient signposts with distances measured in furlongs (a furlong is an eighth of a mile). Many of the roads serve only the local farms. A local feature are the triangular T-junctions, with grass in the middle. The route heads through Ormiston and Cousland and back to Eskbank.

Places of interest along the route

Ⓐ Dalkeith Country Park, Dalkeith

The country park comprises the extensive grounds of Dalkeith Palace (not open to the public), in an 18th-century planned landscape. There are farm animals, woodland and nature trails. Just inside the gates is St Mary's Church, built as a chapel for Dalkeith Palace in 1843 by William Burn, and containing a hammerbeam roof, fine stained glass, heraldic floor tiles and Scotland's only working water-powered organ. Beyond the church is an adventure playground, and beyond this, the Ice House, the Stable Block (with gift shop and café in an attractive cobbled courtyard), the Orangery and the Laundry House, now used as offices. Ranger service. Picnic area. Open April to September, daily 1000–1800. Charge. Telephone 0131 654 1666.

Poppy field, East Lothian

B Pencaitland

Divided by the Tyne Water, Pencaitland has a fine three-arched bridge, dating from 1510. The village contains many picturesque buildings, including the Caledonian Arms, an old coach stop with stables at the rear, Hope Cottage with a grand wrought-iron gateway, and the Old Smiddy, now a pub and restaurant. The war memorial was designed by Robert Lorimer, a famous domestic architect. An information board by the church gives information on places of interest in the village. The tiny pan-tiled house at the church entrance is where the church elders sat, to take the collection from the parishioners.

C Glenkinchie Distillery, near Pencaitland

This is the only remaining malt whisky distillery close to Edinburgh. Visitors can see all aspects of the traditional craft of whisky distillation, from malt storage to warehousing. Exhibition, gift shop and picnic area. Open May to September, Monday–Saturday 0930–1600, Sunday 1200–1600; October to April, Monday–Friday 0930–1600. Charge. Telephone (01875) 342004.

D Cousland Smiddy, Cousland

There has been a blacksmith in Cousland since 1703. The Smiddy is still in use, preserved by the Smiddy Trust, and the owner will happily show visitors around.

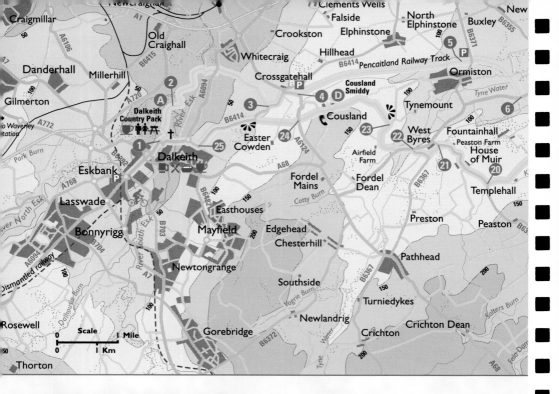

Route description

From Eskbank roundabout take the A6094 Eskbank Road, SP Dalkeith. Continue SO through town centre passing three sets of lights, SP A6094 Musselburgh.

1   SO, where the main road goes sharp right, on cobbled road through gates of Dalkeith Country Park. Immediately on right is St Mary's Church. Continue SO downhill to stable block, passing adventure playground on left. Keep left around stable block and pass orangery.

2.5km (1.5 miles)

2   Cross River Esk and continue SO for 2 km (1 mile). RHF at grassy triangular junction, exit park through gates and TL onto A6094 (with care). TR at TJ onto minor road, SP Smeaton Farm, for steady climb.

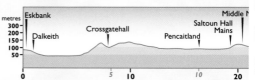

3   TL at TJ, blue SP Ormiston (6km/3.5 miles). Continue to Crossgatehall where bear right at traffic lights onto A6124, Pathhead Road, SP Ormiston.

4   TL onto track, SP Ormiston. This is the start of the Pencaitland Railway Track, with car park and information board. Continue on track through tree-lined valley – beware, the surface is quite poor in places with muddy patches. Along way, concrete posts indicate where there were coal mines. RHF at slag heaps.

5   Pass Ormiston Station, now marked by car park and bridge leading to Ormiston village

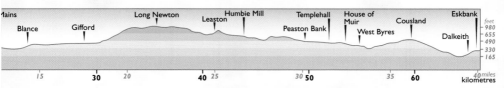

(11.5 km/7 miles). After bridge, RHF past huge silo.

6 Track leads up to A6093. Cross with care and continue on track which runs parallel to road, towards Pencaitland.

7 TL at another huge silo and follow track to main road, where TR into Pencaitland (13.5km/8.5 miles). Go SO, crossing Tyne Water. On right is Pencaitland Church, with information board. Continue. ***16km (10 miles)***

8 TR at XR at war memorial (picnic spot), SP East Saltoun B6355. Pass Saltoun Hall Mains (farm), then TL off B6355.

9 TR at TJ at double bend onto small winding road, no SP but grassy triangular junction (19.5km/12 miles). Pass East Blance Farm. View to north of Lomond Hills in Fife.

10 TL at TJ onto B6355, no SP, and SO at XR, SP Gifford B6355. Road now enters wooded section for about 2km (1 mile) and is well sheltered. Road then dips and rises. Continue on B6355 to Gifford. ***26km (16 miles)***

11 To visit Gifford, follow main road into village. Otherwise, turn half right at XR, SP Longyester, for steady climb into the Lammermuir Hills. SO at TJ, SP Longyester.

12 Arrive Longyester. TR at TJ (or SO to see ancient SP in trees, with distance in furlongs). Continue into Long Newton on wooded, sheltered road. Views of Traprain Law, North Berwick Law, Lomond Hills, and eventually, of Arthur's Seat and Pentlands.

13 Arrive Long Newton (row of houses and phone box). TL (effectively SO) at TJ, no SP (30.5km/19 miles). Pass Kidlaw Farm and SO at junction, SPStobshiel and Leaston. Continue and pass Stobshiel Farm on left. Road bears right, then descends.

14 Easy to miss – TL at TJ, no SP (triangular junction). Continue through Leaston.

15 Keep right as road climbs after Leaston, SP No Through Road Ahead.

16 TL at TJ onto B6368, SP Dalkeith. Continue. The road now runs straight, but undulating, between high beech hedges. **40km (25 miles)**

17 Continue SO on B6371 at XR by war memorial, SP Ormiston. Road descends steeply to the Keith Water – take care, broken surface in parts. Then climb.

18 RHF near top of hill, no SP (old SP at junction has no arms). TR at TJ, SP Saltoun Station. Continue for 1km (0.6 mile).

19 Easy to miss – TL at TJ, no SP (view of line of pylons about 1km/0.6 mile ahead). Continue as road descends through Peaston Bank, passes Glenkinchie Distillery on right, then climbs again. TL at TJ, no SP.

20 TR at TJ onto B6371, SP Ormiston (50km/ 31 miles). Pass Peaston Farm and cross stream.

21 Easy to miss – TL at TJ (as road starts to rise, beside stone wall) onto minor road. Pass West Byres. TR at TJ onto B6367, no SP.

22 TL at TJ for 200m, SP Dalkeith A6093. TR at TJ onto minor road, no SP (crash barriers on right on both sides of junction). RHF by Airfield Farm entrance.

23 TL at TJ, SP Cousland, for steady climb up to village. Extensive views to east. Pass school and phone box. To visit Cousland Smiddy, TR onto track, small SP Cousland Smithy (56km/35 miles). Otherwise, continue through village and SO at TJ near end of village. Steep descent to XR with A6124 – take care.

24 SO at XR, SP Dalkeith. Short, steep climb for great views to Pentland Hills. LHF (effectively SO), SP Smeaton to right.

25 TR at TJ, SP Dalkeith B6414. TL at round-about, SP Dalkeith A6094. Continue to town centre where SO at all junctions to Eskbank and the end of the route. **64km (40 miles)**

Food and drink

Plenty of choice in Dalkeith, with two cafés on South Street. There are pubs at Gifford, and an excellent bakery. Humbie has a convenience store. Refreshments are also available at Dalkeith Country Park.

Caledonian Arms, Pencaitland
Morning coffee and bar lunches served.

Old Smiddy, Pencaitland
Bar meals available.

Village Shop, Pencaitland
Sells filled rolls, hot and cold snacks and ice cream.

Goblin Ha', Gifford
Bar meals available at this pub with secure bicycle parking.

Tweeddale Arms, Gifford
Morning coffee and bar lunches offered.

Village Hall, Gifford
Teas served (for charity fundraising) on Sunday afternoons in summer.

HAWICK AND THE ETTRICK VALLEY

Route information

 Distance   70.5km (44 miles)

Grade   Strenuous

Terrain   Virtually traffic-free roads with three significant climbs. Suitable for all bicycles with gears to cope with the hills.

Time to allow   6 hours.

Getting there by car   Hawick lies 81km (50.5 miles) south of Edinburgh on the A7. Park at Wilton Park – from the A7 at the south end of town, follow SP Wilton Park at mini round-about. Cross river and car park is on left.

Getting there by train   There is no practical rail access to this route but some buses between Edinburgh and Hawick will carry bicycles. For information, telephone Lowland Buses on 0131 663 1945.

Through the Borders country, taking in hills and valleys. From Hawick, the route starts with a ride up the gentle valley of Borthwick, followed by substantial climbing. Then a descent into the Ettrick valley, and the route follows the Ettrick Water. With a climb over Woll Rig and further descent you arrive in Ashkirk, from where the route returns to Hawick via another summit, Blawearie. The scenery varies from pastoral to forest, moorland and reservoir and the virtually traffic-free roads make for excellent cycling.

Places of interest along the route

Ⓐ Hawick

Drumlanrig's Tower is a former 15th-century stronghold of the Douglas family. Visitor centre and gift shop. Open March to October, Monday–Saturday 1000–1700, Sunday 1200–1700; until 1730 in June and September and until 1800 in July and August. Charge. Telephone (01450) 377615. **Wilton Park** comprises 43ha (107 acres) of extensive shrubberies and mature trees. Tearoom and picnic areas. Open all year, daily 0730–1600. Telephone (01450) 378023. In the grounds of the park are **Hawick Museum**, containing displays on local history, and the **Scott Art Gallery**, housing 19th- and 20th-century Scottish art. Also Jimmy Guthrie contemporary motor-cycling exhibition. Open April to September, Monday–Friday 1000–1200 and 1300–1700, Saturday and Sunday 1400–1645; October to March, Monday–Friday 1300–1600, Saturday and Sunday 1400–1600. Charge. Telephone (01450) 373457.

Ⓑ Redfordgreen School

The site of the school, opposite the entrance to Craik Forest, is marked by a cairn which records that the school existed from 1885 to 1955 – a symbol of a vanished community in an area now almost uninhabited

Ⓒ Aikwood Tower, near Selkirk

A restored 16th-century tower, housing an exhibition on James Hogg, the Ettrick Shepherd. Open April to September, Tuesday, Thursday and Sunday 1400–1700. Charge. Telephone (01750) 52253.

Route description

From Wilton Park car park, head for the riverside path, SP To Public Park. Join Victoria Road for 100m. SO through park gates as road bears right. Pass museum and art gallery, and follow SP Walled Garden. TL onto Wilton Park Road and pass walled garden.

1 TL (effectively SO) at TJ, keeping beside river.

2 TR at TJ, no SP (bridge on left). Steady climb up valley of Borthwick Water to Roberton (8km/5 miles). Climb begins in earnest. Extensive views in all directions from summit (10.5km/6.5 miles). Continue to Alemoor Loch.

3 Arrive loch and continue on B711. Pass Redfordgreen School – the cairn is opposite entrance to Craik Forest. Continue. After Clearburn, descend into Ettrick Valley and cross Ettrick Water.

4 TR at TJ onto B7009, SP Innerleithen.
27km (17 miles)

5 TR (effectively SO) at TJ, SP Selkirk B7009. Continue for gradual descent down Ettrick valley and through Ettrickbridge.
39.5km (24.5 miles)

6 Continue on B7009 and pass entrance to Aikwood Tower on right. *44km (27.5 miles)*

7 TR at TJ, SP Ashkirk, for hard climb out of valley. *47km (29 miles)*

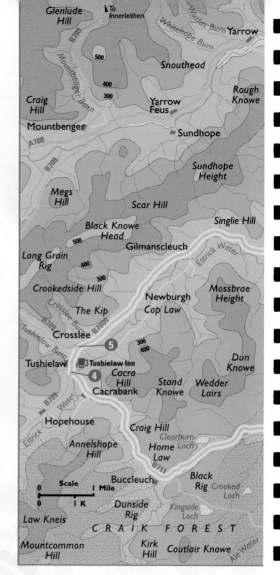

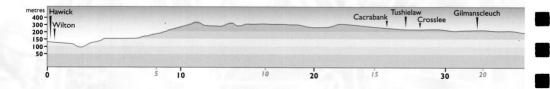

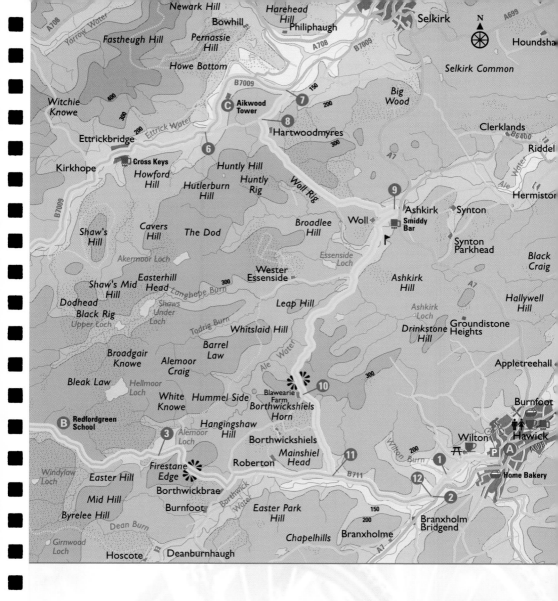

Newark Hill
Harehead Hill
Bowhill
Philiphaugh
Selkirk
Houndsha
Fastheugh Hill
Pernassie Hill
Howe Bottom
A708
B7009
Selkirk Common
Witchie Knowe
B7009
7
150
200
Big Wood
Aikwood Tower
C
Ettrick Water
Clerklands
Riddel
8
Hartwoodmyres
400
300
A7
Ettrickbridge
6
Kirkhope
Cross Keys
Huntly Hill
Huntly Rig
Woll Rig
Ale Water
Hermiston
Howford Hill
Hutlerburn Hill
9
Ashkirk
Synton
Shaw's Hill
Cavers Hill
The Dod
Broadlee Hill
Woll
Smiddy Bar
Synton Parkhead
Black Craig
Akermoor Loch
Essenside Loch
Wester Essenside
Ashkirk Hill
Hallywell Hill
Easterhill Head
Shaw's Mid Hill
Langhope Burn
300
Leap Hill
Ashkirk Loch
Drinkstone Hill
Groundistone Heights
A7
Dodhead
Black Rig
Upper Loch
Shaws Under Loch
Todrig Burn
Whitslaid Hill
Ale Water
Appletreehall
Broadgair Knowe
Barrel Law
Alemoor Craig
Bleak Law
Hellmoor Loch
White Knowe
Hummel Side
Blawearie Farm
Borthwickshiels Horn
10
300
Burnfoot
Burnfoot
Redfordgreen School
B
Hangingshaw Hill
Borthwickshiels
Wilton Burn
200
Wilton
A
Hawick
P
3
Alemoor Loch
Mainshiel Head
11
1
Windylaw Loch
Firestane Edge
Roberton
B711
12
Home Bakery
Easter Hill
Mid Hill
Borthwickbrae
Burnfoot
Borthwick Water
Easter Park Hill
150
200
Branxholm Bridgend
2
Byrelee Hill
Dean Burn
Chapelhills
Branxholme
A7
Girnwood Loch
Hoscote
Deanburnhaugh

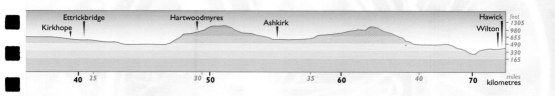

								feet
Ettrickbridge	Hartwoodmyres	Ashkirk				Hawick	1305
Kirkhope						Wilton	980
							655
							490
							330
							165

40   25
30   50
35   60
40
70
miles
kilometres

95

8 TL at TJ, SP Ashkirk. Continue climb. View back of Bowhill House and Park, Ettrick valley and tips of Eildon Hills. Reach summit at 50km (31 miles). Then, long descent, steep in parts, with one sharp left bend.

9 Arrive Ashkirk. TR at TJ, SP Roberton (54km/33.5 miles). Pass Woll Golf Course and continue as road follows valley, crosses Ale Water twice, and climbs steadily. Reach summit at Blawearie Farm beside small clump of forest. Extensive all-round views.

10 TL at TJ, SP Hawick.   *61km (38 miles)*

11 TL at TJ, SP Hawick.

12 TL at TJ, SP Wilton and return to Hawick and car park via Wilton Park.
    70.5km (44 miles)

Typical Borders country

Food and drink

There is plenty of choice in Hawick and refreshments are available at Wilton Park.

Home Bakery, Howegate, Hawick
Serves excellent filled rolls.

Tushielaw Inn, Tushielaw
Meals served at weekends only.

Cross Keys, Ettrickbridge
Morning coffees, lunches and bar meals available.

Smiddy Bar, Ashkirk
Filled rolls available at weekend lunchtimes.

Route 23

MIDLOTHIAN – THE MOORFOOT AND THE PENTLAND HILLS

Route information

Distance 66km (41 miles)

Grade Moderate

Terrain Mostly undulating roads, with a couple of larger hills. The final 10km (6 miles) of the route follows a cycle track along a disused railway, and about half is tarmacked. Suitable for most bicycles with gears to cope with the hills.

Time to allow 6 hours.

Getting there by car Gilmerton is 8km (5 miles) from the centre of Edinburgh. Gilmerton XR is on the A772 Gilmerton Road (old A7), at the junction with the B701. Park by the local shops.

Getting there by train The nearest railway station is Edinburgh Waverley (11km/7 miles from Gilmerton). TL out of the station onto Waverley Bridge. SO at XR (round-about) up Cockburn Street (steep – you might want to walk). TL into High Street and TR (with care) at XR into South Bridge. This is the A701 which you follow through Newington. Then take the A772 all the way to Gilmerton crossroads.

Starting on the outskirts of Edinburgh, this route takes you through the pleasant Midlothian countryside, to the villages of Carrington and Temple, and on to Gladhouse Reservoir and the edge of the Moorfoot Hills, with fine views. Then on to Shiplaw and through Cloich Forest, with views of the Pentlands on one side, the Moorfoots on the other. On across Auchencorth Moss, an area of open moorland, on a straight minor road which can be very fast with a tailwind. Downhill to Penicuik, to follow a section of the Penicuik–Musselburgh Cycleway along a disused railway, through two short tunnels and back to Eskbank.

Food and drink

Lots of choice in Penicuik – the eating places are all close to each other towards the south end of town.

Dobbie's Garden Centre, near Gilmerton
This garden centre, close to the start and finish of the route, has a café.

Scots Pine Restaurant, Eddleston
A 1km (0.6 mile) detour off the route, the café offers morning and afternoon teas, and lunches.

Peni Deli, Penicuik
One of the best choices for refreshment in town.

Olympia Café, Penicuik
Good choice for Italian ice cream.

Route description

From Gilmerton XR, head away from the city along Drum Street. SO at mini roundabout, SP Eskbank.

1 SO over city bypass and past Dobbie's Garden Centre to roundabout, where SO, SP Eskbank. SO at Melville Gate, SP Eskbank. Views of North Esk valley and Glenesk Viaduct.

2 Take third exit at Eskbank roundabout, SP Hardengreen B6392. At next roundabout, TL for 400m, SP Galashiels A7.

3 TR under Lothianbridge Viaduct, onto minor road SP Carrington. *6km (3.5 miles)*

4 SO at Cockpen XR, no SP (Cockpen Church on right). Then, SO at all junctions to Carrington Village.

5 Arrive Carrington. TL, SP Temple.
11km (7 miles)

6 TL across Braidwood Bridge, and TR, SP Temple. Climb steadily through village.

7 TR at TJ, SP Yorkston.

8 SO at TJ in Yorkston (cottages), no SP (16km/10 miles). Then, TR (effectively SO) at TJ and climb. Views from summit of Moorfoot Hills and Gladhouse Reservoir. Follow road as it descends to reservoir.

9 TR sharply at foot of road – gravel on turn, take care. Continue alongside reservoir (nice views and picnic spots).

10 TL at TJ at end of reservoir, SP Moorfoot.

11 TL at TJ, SP Peebles A703. Take care as this road can be busy. *26km (16 miles)*

12 TR at TJ, SP Lamancha. (For Eddleston and café SO on A703 for 1km/0.6 mile.)

13 TR at XR, SP Lamancha. Cycle through Cloich Forest.

14 TL at TJ at Whim Farm onto A701, no SP.
34km (21 miles)

15 TR at TJ, SP Macbiehill. Descend steeply at Macbiehill Farm (double bend at foot – take care).

16 TR at XR, SP Penicuik (40.5km/25 miles). Continue on straight road over Auchencorth Moss.

17 TL at TJ onto A701, no SP.

18 To visit Penicuik, SO at foot of hill (after B6372 junction). Otherwise, to continue route, TR after junction, into residential Valleyfield Road, SP Bonnyrigg (50km/31 miles). After 150m, TR onto cycle track, and cross river twice. After second bridge, (easy to miss) take track on left going up bank, no SP – this is the main track (but the smaller track SO is also possible, but rough). This is part of the Penicuik– Musselburgh Cycleway.

19 Continue through Rosewell and cross main road diagonally to re-join track, which runs parallel to main road. *56.5km (35 miles)*

20 Arrive Bonnyrigg Station (look out for glass on path). Cross main road and continue down residential road opposite (no SP). Cycle track resumes after 150m at end of road.

21 This track ends at Hardengreen, on bridge over A7. TR onto another track for 300m. TL onto tarmacked cycle track.

22 Track ends at Eskbank Station. Go up ramp, past station building onto main road, and TR for 100m. TL (first exit) at Eskbank round-about and return to Gilmerton XR to complete the route. *66km (41 miles)*

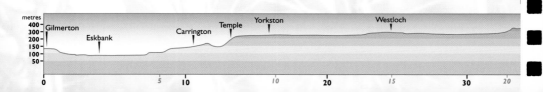

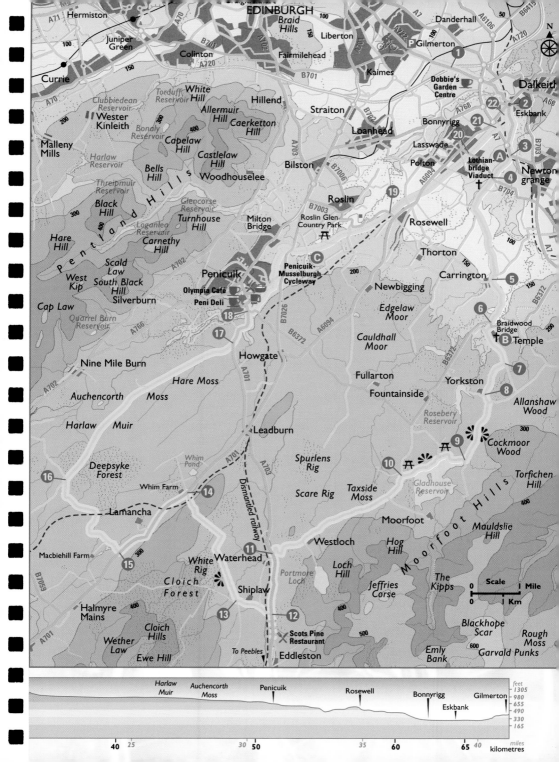

The Pentlands

A Lothianbridge Viaduct, Hardengreen

This magnificent viaduct carried the Waverley Line (Edinburgh to Carlisle via the Borders) across the South Esk, until its closure in 1969. There are plans to restore it as a cycle track, or even as a rail link to Gorebridge.

B Temple

Temple is a charming village of one main street and takes its name from the Knights Templar who had their Scottish headquarters here between the 12th and 14th centuries. The old church, down by the river, dates from the 14th century.

C Penicuik–Musselburgh Cycleway

This route uses the cycleway between Penicuik and Dalkeith, along a disused railway track, and crosses two viaducts. The Firth Viaduct was completed in 1871 and designed by Thomas Bouch, infamous as the designer of the ill-fated Tay Bridge which collapsed in December 1879. The Glenesk Viaduct is a magnificent single-span structure that carried the railway over the River Esk. Starting at the site of the old Valleyfield Paper Mill, the cycleway skirts to the south of Penicuik and follows the River Esk through woods and a tunnel to Dalmore Paper Mill. The cycleway passes south of Roslin Glen Country Park, across the site of a gun powder mill, operational between 1800 and 1953. The factory supplied munitions for the Napoleonic, First and Second World Wars, as well as explosives for the coal mining industry. Some of the buildings still survive, together with remains of the corrugated iron used to minimise the effects of a possible explosion. The cycleway also passes through an area of ancient woodland, home to a wide variety of wildlife. For further information, telephone the Countryside Ranger on (01875) 821990.

MOFFAT AND ESKDALE

Route information

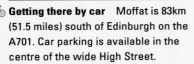

Distance 89.5km (55.5 miles)

Grade Strenuous

Terrain Gentle gradients for the first few miles, then some long climbs and corresponding descents. The last 20km (12.5 miles) are mainly downhill. There is a 5km (3 mile) section of off-road, with a steep descent, at the end. Suitable for most bicycles with gears to cope with the hills.

Time to allow 7 hours.

Getting there by car Moffat is 83km (51.5 miles) south of Edinburgh on the A701. Car parking is available in the centre of the wide High Street.

Getting there by train The nearest railway station is at Lockerbie. To join the route at Boreland (10.5km/6.5 miles away), TR out of station and follow B723, SP Boreland/Eskdalemuir into Boreland. Start the route by continuing on B723 through village at direction 4. Some buses between Edinburgh and Moffat will carry bicycles. For further information, telephone Stagecoach Express on (01387) 253496.

This route starts in Moffat, in Dumfries and Galloway, and travels into the Borders. It is a ride of great variety, both in scenery – pastoral countryside, forest, moorland, the wild upper valley of Moffat Water, and lochs large (St Mary's) and small (picturesque Loch Tima) – and terrain, from gentle to rugged. The roads used are all quiet.

Places of interest along the route

A Moffat

Moffat has long been a popular tourist centre. In the 17th century, it was known as the 'Cheltenham of Scotland', when its sulphur springs were popular. The **Moffat Museum**, Church Gate, is located in an old bakehouse. The museum describes the history of the area, the people, border raids, Covenanters, education, sports and pastimes, and famous people. Gift shop. Open Easter and May to September, Monday–Saturday (except Wednesday afternoon) 1030–1300 and 1430–1700, Sunday 1430–1700. Charge. Telephone (01683) 220868. At **Tweedhope Sheep Dogs**, Selkirk Road, visitors can see Border Collies work and train in a scenic environment. Gift shop. Open Easter to October, daily 1100–1200 and 1500–1600. Charge. Telephone (01683) 221471.

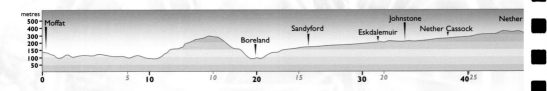

St Mary's Loch

B Samye Ling Tibetan Centre, Eskdalemuir

A magnificent Tibetan temple in traditional Buddhist style, in beautiful surroundings. Gardens and riverside walks. Gift shop, café and picnic area. Open all year: temple 0600–2200, café 0900–1700, shop 1030–1700. Admission by donation. Telephone (013873) 73232.

C James Hogg Monument, by Ettrick

A monument on the site of the birthplace of James Hogg (1770–1835). Known as the Ettrick Shepherd, Hogg was a friend of Scott and author of *Confessions of a Justified Sinner*. His grave is in the nearby church. Access at all reasonable times. Free.

D St Mary's Loch

Beautifully set among smooth green hills, this 4.5km (3 mile) long loch is used for sailing and fishing. On the neck of land separating it from Loch of the Lowes, at the south end, stands Tibbie Shiel's Inn. The inn was kept by Tibbie Shiel (Elizabeth Richardson, 1783–1878) from 1823 and was a meeting place for many 19th-century writers. Beside the road towards the north end of the loch is a seated statue of James Hogg (see C).

E Grey Mare's Tail

Spectacular 61m (200 feet) waterfall in landscape of geological interest and rich in wildflowers. Herd of wild goats. Ranger service. National Trust for Scotland property. Open all year at all reasonable times. Telephone (01556) 502575.

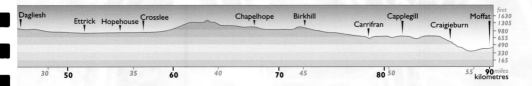

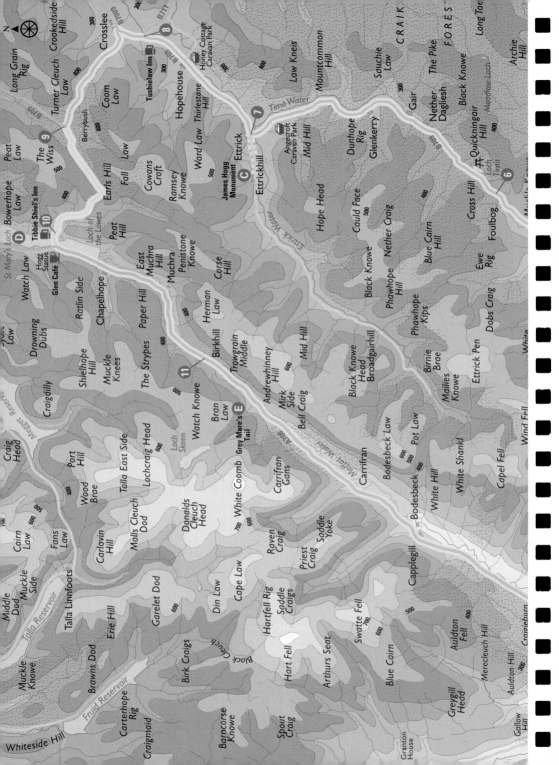

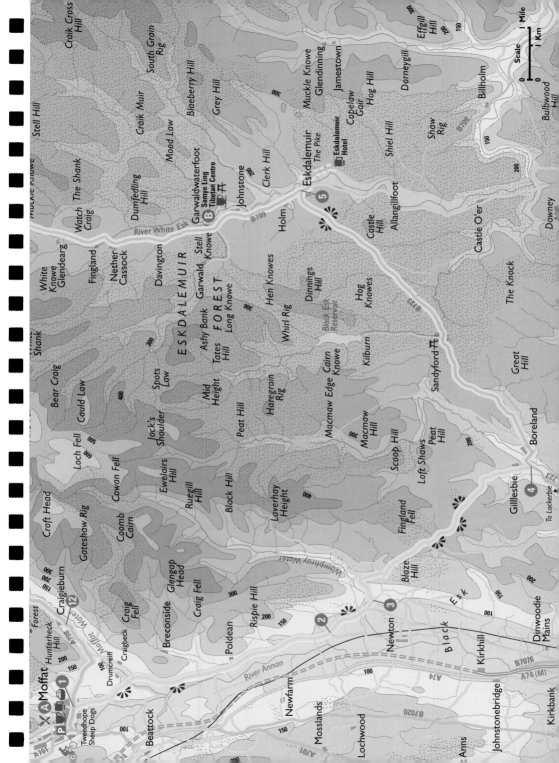

Route description

Head to south end of High Street (slightly downhill) and TL onto A708, SP Selkirk. Pass Tweedhope Sheep Dogs on right.

1 TR at TJ onto old Carlisle Road, SP Boreland. LHF at junction, SP Wamphray (1.5km/1 mile). Views to right of Lowther Hills and, in far distance, the Lake District and the Solway Firth. Descend and cross Moffat Water for gentle climb.

2 Take LHF, SP Boreland. ***9km (5.5 miles)***

3 TL at TJ, SP Boreland (11km/7 miles). First summit reached at 15.5km (9.5 miles). Continue on this undulating road.

4 TL at TJ, SP Eskdalemuir B723 (19km/ 12 miles). Continue through Boreland, into forest. Pass Forest Enterprise picnic spot at Sandyford. Exit forest and descend to Eskdalemuir.

5 Arrive Eskdalemuir. To visit Eskdalemuir Hotel, TR for 1.5km (1 mile). Otherwise, TL at TJ, SP Ettrick B709 (32km/20 miles). Pass Samye Ling Tibetan Centre on right (34.5km/21.5 miles). Continue on B709, cross River White Esk and climb steadily.

6 At summit cross Dumfries & Galloway/ Borders boundary (42.5km/26.5 miles). Enter forest. Pass Loch Tima (picnic spot). Continue for long, steady descent alongside Tima Water and pass Angecroft Caravan Park. ***50.5km (31.5 miles)***

7 Cross Ettrick Water. To visit James Hogg Monument, TL at junction for 1.5km (1 mile). Otherwise, bear right at TJ, SP Innerleithen. Pass Honey Cottage Caravan Park on right after hump back bridge. Views of Ettrick Valley ahead.

8 Arrive Tushielaw Inn (56km/35 miles). TL at TJ, SP Innerleithen B709. Climb steadily, past Berrybush.

9 At summit, TL onto track as road veers right, SP Unsafe Bridge (61km/38 miles). Continue

on track as it enters and leaves forest and bends right. Southern Upland Way (long distance footpath) comes in from left. Steep descent.

10 Arrive St Mary's Loch. Track ends at gate. Continue SO and pass Tibbie Shiel's Inn on right (66km/41 miles). Exit to main road (A708) where TL, no SP. Hogg Statue on hill ahead. Continue past Chapelhope for steady climb.

11 Arrive summit and Borders/Dumfries and Galloway boundary (72.5km/45 miles). Continue and pass Grey Mare's Tail (74.5km/ 46.5 miles). Continue on A708 towards Moffat.

12 Pass Craigieburn Forest on right (85km/53 miles), and continue into Moffat, to the High Street and the end of the route.
89.5km (55.5 miles)

Food and drink

Moffat is geared for tourism and there are several tearooms, bakeries and pubs in the High Street, all close together. There is a restaurant at Moffat Woollen Mill, in the town. There are convenience stores at Angecroft Caravan Park, before Ettrick, and at Honey Cottage Caravan Park, just after Ettrick. Refreshments are available at the Samye Ling Tibetan Centre.

Eskdalemuir Hotel, Eskdalemuir
Bar meals served, 1.5km (1 mile) off the route.

Tushielaw Inn, Tushielaw
Meals served at weekends only.

Tibbie Shiel's Inn, St Mary's Loch
Bar meals, lunches and high teas available.

Glen Café, St Mary's Loch
Tea, coffee, sandwiches and snacks served.

Route 25 — EDINBURGH TO THE BORDERS – A GRANDE RANDONNÉE

Route information

Distance   113km (70 miles)

Grade   Moderate

Terrain   Hilly in parts, but route mostly follows valley roads. There are two short off-road sections, suitable for most bicycles.

Time to allow   8–9 hours.

Getting there by car   The start of the route, Fairmilehead XR, is 7km (4.5 miles) south of Edinbugh city centre, at the junction of the A702 and B701. There is limited parking by the Church Hall, just east of the XR, off the B701 on Frogston Avenue. Otherwise, park in the residential streets.

Getting there by train   The nearest railway station is Edinburgh Waverley, 11km (7 miles) from Fairmilehead. TR out of station onto Waverley Bridge. TL and cycle all way along Princes Street. TL at traffic lights into Lothian Road (A702). Stay on this road all the way to Fairmilehead, following SP A702.

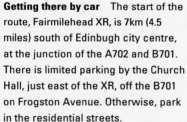

The route takes in Edinburgh, Midlothian and the Borders, and dips twice into East Lothian. It will take you through the scenic valleys of the Lyne, the Tweed, the Leithen and Heriot Waters, the historic towns of Peebles and Innerleithen and unspoilt villages such as Heriot and Crichton.

Places of interest along the route

A Neidpath Castle, near Peebles

Neidpath Castle is a rare example of a 14th-century castle, converted into a tower house in the 17th century. See route 20 for details.

B Peebles

Peebles is a traditional Borders town, on the River Tweed. For details, see route 20.

C Kailzie Gardens, near Peebles

The gardens covers 7ha (17 acres). There is a walled garden created in 1812, rose garden, greenhouses, woodland and burnside walks, duck pond and an art gallery. Gift shop, tea-room and picnic area. Open March to October, daily 1100–1730; November to February, daily 1100–dusk. Charge. Telephone (01721) 720007.

D Traquair House, Innerleithen

This 12th-century house, home of the Stuarts, is said to be the oldest continuously inhabited house in Scotland. In the grounds are craft workshops, a maze and 18th-century brew-house (which still produces beer). Also woodland and River Tweed walks. Motorists have to pay to enter the grounds, but cyclists can use the side entrance off the B709 (see route). Tearoom. Open April, May and September, daily 1230–1730; June to August, daily 1030–1730; October, Friday and Saturday 1230–1730. Charge. Telephone (01896) 830323.

E Robert Smail's Printing Works, Innerleithen

A National Trust for Scotland property, this restored printing works uses the machinery and methods of the early 20th century. Visitors can watch the printer at work and try setting type by

Tranent
Macmerry
A199
B6355
B6371
Ormiston
To Haddington
House of Muir
B6371
Rose Mains
Pathhead
The Foresters
Emmaus Coffee Lounge
Crichton
Saughland
B6458
Tynehead
Cowbraehill
Brothershiels
400
Dismantled railway
300
Musselburgh
Wallyford
Clements Wells
Elphinstone
B1348
B6414
Crossgatehall
Whitecraig
A6093
B6367
B6367
Cousland
Southfield
Chesterhill
Fordel Mains
A68
B6414
A6124
Crichton
B6367
Tynehead
Middleton Moor
Middleton
Falahill
Heriot Cleugh
Shoestanes
B7007
Inveresk
Joppa
Niddrie
Newcraighall
Old
Craighall
Newton
B6415
A720
Smeeton Farm
A6094
Dalkeith
B6482
Easthouses
Mayfield
Newtongrange
Arniston Engine
Newlandrig
B6372
Gorebridge
North Middleton
Windy Law
Ford
Allanshaw Wood
Cockmoor Wood
Torfichen Hill
Duddingston
Craigmillar
A7
A6106
Danderhall
Libberton
Gilmerton
A772
Eskbank
Lasswade
Bonnyrigg
B704
Polton
B703
River South Esk
Carrington
Temple
B6372
Rosebery Reservoir
Edgelaw Reservoir
300
400
EDINBURGH
Morningside
Gracemount
Kaimes
Loanhead
Bilston
Straiton
Polton
Rosewell
Thorton
Newbigging
Edgelaw Moor
Cauldhall Moor
Fullarton
Fullarton Water
B6372
Taxside
Gladhouse
Waverley Holyrood Station Park
Braid Hills
Fairmilehead
P
Roslin
Auchendinny
Milton Bridge
Dismantled Railway
Howgate
B7026
Spurlens Rig
Scare Rig
Leadburn
A703
Morningside
Craiglockhart
A701
A702
Hillend
Caerketton Hill
Castlelaw Hill
Woodhouselee
Glencorse Resr
Boghall Burn
Penicuik
Hare Moss
Auchencorth Moss
Whim Pond
Dismd
Corstorphine
Juniper Green
Colinton
A720
Torduff Reservoir
Clubbiedean Reservoir
Bonaly Reservoir
Allermuir Hill
Capelaw Hill
Bells Hill
Turnhouse Hill
Carnethy Hill
Scald Law
Loganlea Resr
Quarrel Burn Reservoir
Nine Mile Burn
Hare Moss
Deepsyke Forest
Edinburgh Airport
Gogar
Ratho Station
Hermiston
Currie
Balerno
Malleny Mills
Warklaw Hill
Wester Kinleith
Harlaw Reservoir
Threipmuir Reservoir
Black Hill
Hare Hill
West Kip
Green Law
Kitchen Moss
Cock Rig
Low Spittal Hill
Carlops
Harlaw Muir
Dalmahoy Hill
Ratho
Cockburn
Cockburnhill
East Cairn Hill
Mid Hill
Deerhope Rig
Baddinsgill Reservoir
Mount Maw
Faw Mount
M8
Union Canal
50
1
100
150
200
300
N

Corsehope Haltree
Over Shiels
Gately Rig
Great Law
Caddon Water
Darny Burn
Cauld Face
To Galashiels
A72
Heriot
Corsehope Burn
Conely Burn
Calfhope Burn
Scroof Hill
Black Law
Southerly Nick
Holylee
Elibank Law
Ashiesteel Hill
Dod Law
Windy Knowe
Dun Law
Ewes Water
Weather Law
Deaf Heights
Caddon Head
Redscar Law
Maiden Law
Seathope Law
Stony Knowe
Glenhopeknowe Burn
Walkerburn
Dismantled railway
River Tweed
Far Hill
Bold Burn
Glenkinnon Burn
Ladyside
Ladyside Burn
Dewar Hill
Ladyside Height
Eastside Heights
Blackhopebyre
Windlestraw Law
Bareback Knowe
Glede Knowe
Colquhar
Priesthope Hill
Walker Burn
Kirnie Law
Innerleithen
Robert Smail's Printing Works
Elibank and Traquair Forest
Bold Rig
Pipers Knowe
B709
Dewar
Rough Moss
Middle Hill
Whitehope Law
Leithen Hopes
300 400 500
Dod Hill
B709
Leithen Water
St. Ronan's Wells
St. Ronan's Hotel
Traquair House
Traquair
B709
Kirkhouse
Mauldslie Hill
The Kipps
Blackhope Scar
Garvald Punks
Totto Hill
Whinlaws Burn
600
Craig Hope
Black Knowe
Lee Pen
Gardrona
400 300 200
A72
Howford Farm
Quair Water
Kailzie Law
Kirkhope Law
Orchard Rig
Reservoir
Moss
River South
Emly Bank
Jeffries Corse
Cardon Law
Bowbeat Hill
Makeness Kipps
Dunslair Heights
Black Law
Horsburgh Burn
Cardie Hill
Kirn Law
B7062
Cardrona Forest
Glensax Burn
Birkscairn Hill
Loch Burn
Westloch
Loch Hill
Hog Hill
Hog Hill Knowes
Eddleston
Whiteside Edge
Collie Law
Leithen Water
Soonhope Burn
500 400
Glentress Forest
Kittlegairy
Kittlegairy Hill
Glentress
Kailzie Gardens
Kirkburn
Preston Law
Hundleshope Heights
Stob Law
Portmore Loch
300 200
Redscarhead
Pebbles
Kings Muir
Cademuir Hill
Hundleshope Burn
A703
Dismantled railway
Eddleston Water
Neidpath Castle
River Tweed
Kirkton Manor
Woodhouse
Castlehill
Canada Hill
Glenrath Hill
White Rig
Waterheads
Wormiston
Cringletie Hill
White Meldon
South Head Hill
Edston Hill
Lyne Station
Preston Law
Whim Farm
Midlothian Burn
Halmyre Mains
Cloich Hill
Wether Law
Ewe Hill
Kilrubie Hill
Crailzie Hill
Black Meldon
Lyne
A72
Whitelaw Hill
Hunt Law
Breach Law
B7059
Lamancha
Dead Burn
Romannobridge
B7059
B701
Tarth Water
Lyne Water
Penvalla
Hopehead Burn
Stobo
Stobo Burn
Weston Burn
Scale 1 Mile
1 Km
0
West Linton
Blyth Muir
Mountain Cross
Cairn Burn
Dismantled railway
Blyth Bridge
Drochil Hill
Castlecraig
Woolshears Hill
Ladyurd Hill
Hammer Head
Trahenna Hill
Westhill Wood
Pykestone Hill
Scawd Law
Drumelzier
B712
Dismantled railway

hand. Reconstructed water wheel. Gift shop. Open Easter and May to September, Monday–Saturday 1000–1300 and 1400–1700, Sunday 1400–1700; October, Saturday 1000–1300 and 1400–1700, Sunday 1400–1700. Charge. Telephone (01896) 830206.

ⓕ St Ronan's Wells, Innerleithen

A spa resort (up steep hill) made famous by Sir Walter Scott, who features largely in the visitor centre. Visitors can sample the waters. Gift shop, tearoom, garden and picnic area. Open Easter to September, daily 1400–1700. Admission free. Telephone (01896) 830660.

Food and drink

There is plenty of choice in Penicuik, Peebles and Innerleithen. Danderhall, Gilmerton and Gracemount have convenience stores. Refreshments are also available at Kailzie Gardens, Traquair House and St Ronan's Wells.

St Ronan's Hotel, Innerleithen
Bar meals available. Garden.

Emmaus Coffee Lounge, Pathhead
Tea, coffee and home baking in pleasant surroundings.

The Foresters, Pathhead
Pub serving bar meals.

Route description

Start at Fairmilehead XR. Follow A702 down hill, SP Carlisle. Cross city bypass. Take middle road, where road divides into three after Hillend Ski Cenre, SP Peebles A703.

1 TR at roundabout, SP Peebles A701. View of Pentland Hills on right. **5km (3 miles)**

2 SO as road bends right, SP Auchendinny B7026, for steep descent.

3 When road levels, TL to Dalmore Mill, SP Dalmore Mill (7km/4.5 miles). At mill entrance, TR through gate into tunnel. Continue on this track to Penicuik where it ends in small car park. TL into Lower Valleyfield View for 200m.
10.5km (6.5 miles)

4 TL, SP Peebles A701, for steady climb. View of Moorfoot Hills at top. Continue to Leadburn.

5 TR at XR, SP Moffat A701 (15km/9.5 miles). Pass Whim Farm. Views of valley ahead. Gently descend to Romannobridge.

6 TL at TJ, SP Peebles B7059.
22km (13.5 miles)

7 TL at TJ, SP Peebles A72 (27km/17 miles). Pass Lyne Station on right (33km/20.5 miles). Then, pass Neidpath Castle on right and continue into Peebles.

8 To continue into Peebles, TL at roundabout. Otherwise, to continue route, TR (effectively SO) at roundabout, SP Kailzie, (38.5km/24 miles). Cross River Tweed and take LHF, following B7062, SP Kailzie.

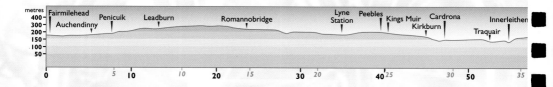

9 Pass entrance to Kailzie Gardens on left (42km/26 miles). Climb, then descend to Cardrona Forest. Pass Howford Farm then Bear Gates and motorists' entrance to Traquair House. *50km (31 miles)*

10 Arrive Traquair village and war memorial. TL at TJ, SP Innerleithen B709. Pass side entrance to Traquair House. Continue on B709. TL at TJ, following main road. Then, LHF into Innerleithen.

11 TR at TJ, SP Galashiels A72. *54.5km (34 miles)*

12 TL at TJ, SP Heriot B709. Continue as road goes through golf course then climbs up Glentress (picnic spots by Leithen Water). Summit reached at 66km (41 miles). Then descend towards Heriot.

13 TR at TJ, SP Heriot and continue on B709 to Heriot village. Cross river. *74km (46 miles)*

14 TL at TJ, SP Edinburgh A7. Take care as this road can be busy. *77km (48 miles)*

15 TR at TJ, SP Pathhead B6367 (80.5km/ 50 miles). View of Lomond Hills and Fife ahead. Descend.

16 Cross old railway. TL at old Tynehead Station, SP Crichton. Climb to summit at 84.5km (52.5 miles). Descend steeply to Crichton.

17 TL at TJ for 50m, SP Pathhead. TR at TJ, SP Pathhead.

18 Arrive Pathhead. TR at TJ with care onto A68, no SP (88.5km/55 miles). TL at TJ, SP Haddington B6367.

19 TL at TJ, SP Dalkeith A6093.

20 TR at TJ, SP Cousland (94km/58.5 miles). Climb. At summit A6124 comes in from left – continue SO, no SP. Superb view of Pentland Hills, Arthur's Seat, Leith, Firth of Forth and Lomond Hills. Descend.

21 Bear left at Crossgatehall traffic lights, SP Dalkeith/Whitecraig (98km/61 miles). TR at TJ, SP Whitecraig. Descend, steeply in parts. Pass Smeaton Farm on left.

22 TL at TJ with care onto main road, no SP. After 30m, TR though gates, past lodge, then bear left for 100m. TR for 100m and TL. Cross River Esk and road becomes track. After 150m take RHF.

23 TL at TJ, no SP (103km/64 miles). From here back to Fairmilehead, route follows cyclists' ring route, SP RR on red background. Continue.

24 TR at roundabout, SP Leith A6106. Continue to Newton village, where TL, SP RR. TL at Danderhall mini roundabout, SP RR.

25 TR at TJ with care onto A7, SP RR. *106.5km (66 miles)*

26 TL at TJ, SP Gilmerton B701. Continue SO at all junctions on B701, SP RR, and return to Fairmilehead and the end of the route. *113km (70 miles)*

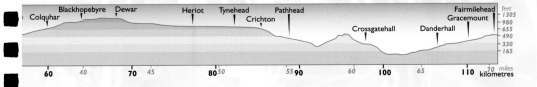

THE CTC

working for cycling

The CTC is Britain's largest national cycling organisation. Founded in 1878, the CTC has over 65,000 members and affiliates throughout the UK, and around 230 local groups. The CTC provides essential services for all leisure cyclists, whether riding on- or off-road, and works to promote cycling and protect cyclists' interests.

Free technical and touring advice

CTC membership makes day-to-day cycling easier. A resident expert cycling engineer answers technical queries about cycle buying, maintenance and equipment. And if you get ambitious about your cycling, the CTC's Touring Department has reams of information about cycling anywhere from Avon to Zimbabwe. Then, when it comes to getting kitted out, the CTC's mail order shop sells a wide variety of clothing and accessories in addition to books, maps and guidebooks, including other titles from HarperCollins Publishers.

CTC Helpdesk – telephone (01483) 417217

CTC members also receive *Cycle Touring and Campaigning* magazine free six times a year. *CT&C* takes pride in its journalistic independence. With reports on cycle trips all over the globe, forensic tests on bikes and equipment, and the most vigorous and effective pro-bike campaigning stance anywhere, *CT&C* is required reading for any cyclist.

CTC membership costs from £15 p.a.

It is not just members who benefit. The CTC works on behalf of all Britain's 22 million cycle owners. Its effective campaigning at national level helped to create the Government's National Cycling Strategy. It is lobbying for lower speed limits on country lanes; campaigning so that you can carry bikes on trains; working with Local Authorities to make towns more cycle-friendly, to ensure that roads are designed to meet cyclists' needs and kept well maintained; making sure that bridleways are kept open; and negotiating cyclists' access to canal towpaths.

Whatever kind of cyclist you are – mountain biker, Sunday potterer, bicycle commuter, or out for the day with your family – cycling is easier and safer with the CTC's knowledge and services in your saddlebag. The CTC is the essential accessory for every cyclist!

For further information contact:
CTC
69 Meadrow
Godalming
Surrey
GU7 3HS

Telephone (01483) 417217
Fax (01483) 426994
e-mail: cycling@ctc.org.uk
Website: http://www.ctc.org.uk